CHANGE

Book 5 of The Witch, the Dragon and the Angel "Trilogy"

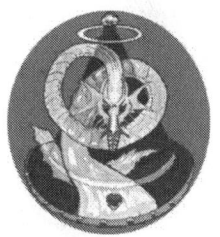

*Titles available in The Witch, the Dragon and the Angel Trilogy
(in reading order):*

Witch Way Home?
Witch Armageddon?
Witch Schism and Chaos?
plus two more (it's a magical trilogy!)
Tsunami
Change

*Related books
(in the same Multiverse)
The Witches' Brew Trilogy:*
Hubble Bubble
Toil
Trouble

And on a similar theme:
Oberon's Bane
Parables from Parallel Places

Coming soon:
Ghost Train, An anthology of short stories

CHANGE
Book 5 of The Witch, the Dragon and the Angel "Trilogy"

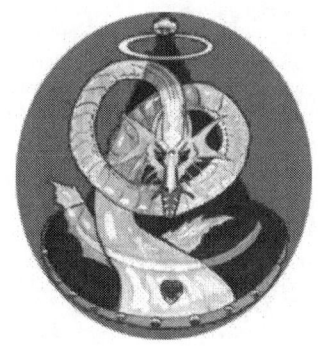

Paul R. Goddard

© Paul Goddard 2015

The right of Paul R Goddard to be identified as the author of this work has been asserted by him in accordance with the Copyright, Designs and Patents Act 1988

All rights reserved. No part of this publication may be reproduced, stored in a retrieval system, or transmitted in any form or by any means, electronic, mechanical, photocopying, recording or otherwise, without prior permission of the copyright owner

All characters in this publication are fictitious and any resemblance to real persons, living or dead, is purely coincidental.

First published in the UK 2015

ISBN 978-1-85457-072-7

Published by: Clinical Press Ltd., Redland Green Farm, Redland, Bristol, BS6 7HF, UK.

Innumerable thanks are again due to Jem, Allan, Liz and Lois. Thank you!

Cover Photograph: Elsa the Giant Pacific Octopus at the Bristol Aquarium, photographed by Aquarist Jake Graham.

Prologue

Alan could not believe his eyes. The girl was undoubtedly beautiful and she had invited him to her hotel room. They had only bumped into each other an hour before when Alan had returned to his temporary abode after attending a conference. The meeting had been just a tad boring and he had got back to the hotel early in the afternoon, missing the last session. Tomorrow would be the final day of the conference then home.

Alan, a large, strong man who liked action rather than inactivity, had been expecting a rather boring evening, perhaps a little reading of the meeting abstracts then an early night. But that was clearly about to change.

After chatting to the gorgeous girl in the bar, where he was having a coffee, she had suggested a more intimate drink in her room. He was now looking round her suite with admiration. It had to be one of the largest in the hotel which was saying something....the hotel was expensive.

'With or without ice?' she asked from the well-stocked bar in the suite.

'Err, with,' replied Alan. 'Definitely with!'

The girl gave a tinkling laugh as if Alan had said something really amusing. She was wearing just a dressing gown and as she laughed it swung slightly apart revealing her slim, tanned thighs, her firm stomach and a glimpse of even more to come.

She really fancies me, thought the big man. *She's definitely into me. This is great.*

The beautiful girl carried the drinks over to Alan. He took a sip from the exotic cocktail she had prepared for him.

'I like it on the rocks, too,' the girl whispered in intimate

2

tones as she led Alan towards the bed.

*

The drink was having a strange effect on Alan. At least he thought it must be the drink.

When he reached the bed all that he wanted to do was to lie out and sleep. The room was spinning slowly and the girl's hair was looking wild.....and a weird blue-green colour with patches that were almost ultramarine.

Something hallucinogenic in the cocktail, thought Alan.

He stared closer at the girl as she reached out and took hold of his hand, singing as she did so. To his horror her mouth had widened impossibly, the teeth had turned into sharp yellow daggers and the tongue was protruding like a giant tentacle with a hollow sucker at its tip.

He was powerless to move as the creature pulled firstly his hand and then his entire right arm into its maw then chomped down on the limb.

There was no sensation of pain.

The mouth pulled free again.

'Turn and change,' mewled the giant maw and, for just a brief moment, the beautiful woman was standing there again.

It's just a bad trip, thought the big man as his other arm disappeared in like manner.

It was only when the monster had almost completely swallowed his body and was digesting his neck that Alan, in a dying moment of lucidity, realised that this might be reality and not a drug-crazed dream.

By then it was too late, far too late.

Chapter 1

Timothy Cranbrook shook himself and tried to wake up. This was difficult in the dim light of the activity room of the residential home in Bristol.

Activity is a euphemism, thought Tim. *Not one of us is up for real activity. All we do is watch TV and sleep.*

The care facility had not been Timothy's first choice. He had wanted to go to a different home which he knew employed two full-time staff just for entertainment and also engaged in active rehabilitation. They had no spare room as yet, though they had put him on the waiting list.

Tim remembered that he had been injured in an industrial accident.

It all seemed a lot easier when I was a teenager, thought Tim. *Fit, healthy and none of this supernatural crap to complicate matters.*

Timothy tried to watch the television but the programme chosen by the carers did not entertain him. He glanced around the room at the other patients. When he looked directly at them they looked fine but from the corner of his eye they seemed to be staring at him with hungry eyes and cannibal teeth. This was not the first time he had noticed their peculiar appearance and he wondered whether it was a side effect of his injury.

Shaking off the weird sensation he focussed again on the TV, shuffled back in his wheelchair and considered his situation.

As far as he could remember Tim's accident had been due to the use of an industrial hex. The business world had quickly caught on to the potential of magic in the workplace. *Thaumaturgical input* was the euphemistic term employed but industrial magic was what most people called it. Nobody yet understood the science of magic but that did not prevent people using it. To be fair to the proponents of industrial magic nobody really seemed to understand quantum mechanics but that did not prevent people using that in numerous applications.

But crucially quantum mechanics was statistically predictable whilst magic was not. Initially manufacturers had been delighted with the way that magic could be used to summons anything apparently from nowhere. Magic goods were sold worldwide. Magic cars, magic clothes, even magic houses.

When parts had disappeared as suddenly as they had been conjured the magic began to be distrusted. Nobody liked to walk down the sidewalk in their best suit only to find that they were standing naked in front of everybody. Or to be driving in their car and find that the steering wheel vamoosed, the windscreen skedaddled and the engine had scarpered ....on a pair of spindly and very hairy legs. So laws had been passed limiting the use of magic in industry solely to enhancing spells......colours, smells, flexibility but not structural components.

Timothy was pretty certain that he had been affected by a feedback loop in which the hex, put on to make the rubber in Wellington boots more flexible, had expanded exponentially and destroyed the moulds the rubber was being poured into. Timothy had been told that he was investigating the equipment when he was blasted by the hex. His skeleton had become too flexible, his spine had whiplashed and he was now partially paralysed from the neck down.

The financial compensation had been immense but the outcome dire. As he sat in the activity room he ruminated that he would, of course, give up all the money for a healthy spine. Anybody would.

Tim tried to wiggle his toes just like he had tried a thousand times before. Nothing. No movement, no sensation. Then he tried moving his right hand....nothing. His left hand worked but the strength had initially been reduced, something he had worked hard on reversing and now the arm was stronger than ever. He had always been right handed but needs must. He now did everything with his strong left hand.

An item on the news caught his attention.

-Police are searching for a missing doctor. Dr. Alan Malova, an internationally famous neurologist, has been missing for almost a week. He was last seen at a hotel in Glasgow where he was attending a conference. His absence was noted the day after he was last seen because he did not attend a session where he had been expected to act as the chairman. A divorced father of two children Alan is aged 43, six foot two in height....

Just as he was getting interested in the broadcast one of the staff members turned the programme over to a banal quiz game entitled Pact and Ready to Go in which today's contestants had to choose a contract for a plane ticket with an airline, guessing what the extra charges would be. The nearest to the figure would be the winner. Tomorrow it would probably be a house and the next day a car.

*

'How are we today?' asked Dick.

Tim looked at the speaker. Dick was the only friend he had made in the care home and he was visiting Tim in his room as he did at least once every day. The man was a volunteer helper, not an inmate, as Tim thought of himself and the others. So Dick was really an unpaid member of staff. His real name, as he reminded people, was Peter Whittington but he was always called Dick for obvious reasons related to the mayoralty of London and various pantomimes that usually involved a cat.

Tim did not particularly like most of the staff. They tended to be rather rough though, on the plus side, none of them were directly cruel. What was particularly galling to Tim was the way that some of them treated him as if he was stupid. He was a very big man, physically disabled, yes, but not mentally damaged. He knew that the other nursing home had a much better reputation but there was still no room.

Dick was the one who was looking into the move for him. Tim trusted him more than he did the other staff...after all Dick, a volunteer, could always move to the other home and continue to be his friend if he wanted to.

'Not bad, considering,' replied Tim. 'But people here are very strange.'

'Well, it's just about to get a bit better,' remarked Dick. 'Your move to the other home is imminent.'

Great, thought Tim. *But I'll miss Dick.*

'Will I see you there?' he asked nervously, afraid of a rebuff.

'I'll definitely visit you at the new home,' smiled the voluntary helper. 'It's just a pity that we've not been able to do more for you whilst you have been here.

Tim looked round at the other people in the activity room. Once again the impression of a room full of cannibals had crept up on him. Even Dick had sharp pointed teeth. Then the sensation faded and normality returned.

Using his one good arm Tim used a hoist to swing himself onto the bed. He needed a rest, his back was playing up again. The strength in his one useful arm was prodigious and he marvelled that he was able to lift himself the way that he did. The doctors had told him that he would gradually regain some usefulness in his other limbs but so far that had not happened.

Perhaps the activity at the other home will help? wondered Tim as he lay back on the bed. *This place is doing nothing for me.*

*

- A police spokesman has told us that the missing doctor, Alan Malova, is just one of a series of professional people who have gone missing from recent conferences. We are now taking you to a

reconstruction of the scene where the doctor disappeared. If you have any information please let us know. Telephone......

Tim was watching the CrimeStop programme and, mercifully, nobody had changed the channel this time. With his one working arm he carefully scribbled the CrimeStop contact number. There was an idea that he had forming in his mind and he wanted to talk it over with someone from the police team working on the disappearances. He was sure that he had a clue that might help though his memory was intermittent these days and his mind was clouded.

*

- *Twenty-two professional people, mostly scientists of high repute, have been reported as missing over the last six months. What has that meant to you, as the event organiser?*
- *The supernatural interventions which started five years ago disrupted the usual conference circuit but the meetings were getting back to a semblance of normality. The disappearance of the professors has again meant that conference participation is dropping and more people are using the internet for their continuing professional development.*

A spokesman from an event management firm was talking and his angle was the dire effect the disappearances were having on his business. He was being questioned by a female presenter.

- *And this is your main concern?*
- *It is often difficult to recruit lecturers, particularly if the event is not at an exotic location, so the suggestion that some group may be targeting scientists is not helping us at all.*
- *So what do you think has happened to the scientists?*
- *I've no idea. Maybe they are taking extended leave?*
- *That doesn't seem likely*
- *Maybe not but I do think that the idea that a luddite resistance group is on the prowl is simply scaremongering.*
- *But it is scientists that have gone missing...*

- True. The missing people have not, however, all been scientists. There have also been some clergymen and women who have vanished, a few doctors and one barrister.

-All from meetings?

- Indeed, all of whom were attending conferences, mostly organised by ourselves.

- People go missing all the time. I would like to ask our police spokesperson if this is in any way different from the normal pattern of missing persons reports.

- Thank you Ciara. This is a very uncommon grouping of missing persons.

A policewoman had replied to the presenter.

- In what way and how many people do go missing?

- About 250,000 people go missing each year in the United Kingdom

- That's a huge number...

- That is so. It was, however, even worse during the recent supernatural crises.

- So what makes this different? We are talking about twenty-two people, not a quarter of a million.

- That's right Ciara but none of the twenty-two were homeless, all of them were expected to be in a certain place at a certain time and did not show up. All were between thirty and fifty-five in age, on a good income with a steady job. Several were due to give keynote lectures.....

- More than half, in fact.

The event management spokesman interrupted the policewoman.

- More than half? That's worrying in itself is it not?

- It is, Ciara. So we are appealing to anyone who has any clues, knows anything about the missing people that you think we should know. Please get in touch with the police.

Or telephone us on the usual CrimeStop number ... 0800....

Chapter 2

'Professor,' the female student called out to the lecturer as he strode away from the hall. 'May I have a word with you?'

Fergus G. Smithson stopped in his tracks. The person calling to him was a very attractive young lady and Smithson's one weakness was that he was a lady's man. He adored beautiful women and he loved it when they, in turn adored and worshipped him.

Smoothing his trademark turquoise trousers and putting on a beaming smile he turned to address the student.

'Can I help you?' he asked, disingenuously, fully aware of the charm he was putting on.

'Oh thank you,' gushed the student. 'You see, I am doing a project on sustainability in the built environment and your lecture was absolutely to the point. Especially with regards to limiting the use of magic.'

'Perhaps we should go to the bar to talk,' suggested the professor.

'I'd like that,' purred the student, almost singing. 'I really would.'

'So would I,' grinned the professor.

'Or perhaps a quick walk in the grounds of the hotel?' suggested the student with a wickedly enticing smile. 'The weather has changed for the better again.'

'Certainly,' the professor nodded his agreement. It did not look as if his evening would be as boring as he had originally thought. The student was exactly what he was looking for.

*

'Thank you for calling us,' the large black policeman

introduced himself. 'I'm Dan Williams.'

'An inspector, no less,' muttered Timothy Cranbrook, looking at the man's uniform.

They were sat in Tim's bedroom in the nursing home, Tim on his ripple mattress chair and the policeman on a hard chair in front of him.

'Detective Chief Inspector, in fact,' replied the policeman. 'But I have not had time since my promotion to obtain a new uniform. I don't normally wear one.'

Timothy raised an eyebrow.

'A plainclothes detective who happens to be in uniform?' he queried.

'Yeah,' grinned the policeman, shuffling a little with discomfort. 'Don't feel right in the uniform. I had to go to a ceremony before coming to see you.'

'Not a funeral, I hope?' remarked Cranbrook.

'No, another medal-giving, public relations exercise,' smiled Williams.

Despite his general misgivings when dealing with the police Tim Cranbrook could not stop himself from warming to the big-hearted policeman in front of him. The policeman in return was looking approvingly at the paralysed man. In particular he was impressed with the way that Cranbrook was keeping himself in shape despite his major problems.

'So I'm all ears,' continued the big man. 'How can you help us?'

'I'm very flattered that my phone call should have elicited such a high level response,' replied the crippled man. 'It was simply an observation that I had made, not firm facts.'

'Any help could be useful,' replied the policeman. 'What have you got?'

'I've been watching the news reports about the missing scientists,' replied Timothy. 'But before I give you my idea I'd like to give you some background about myself.'

'Go ahead,' replied the policeman, settling himself back onto the chair.

He was not worried if this took some time or not. At the moment the investigation was going nowhere and it was at times like this, when there were no leads, that any small suggestion might help.

'I'm an investigator from the Department of Works and Pensions,' stated Cranbrook. 'At least I was until the accident six months ago.'

'Investigating what, exactly?' asked the big policeman, leaning forward again, instantly interested.

'Investigating the use of magic in business practice,' replied the semi-paralysed man. 'Seconded to the HSE, The Health and Safety Executive.'

Williams nodded.

'In particular I was pursuing the illegal use of magic in industrial processes,' continued Tim Cranbrook.

'Right...'

Williams was wondering where this was going but it was already very interesting.

'You will recall that in the year after the supernatural interventions had died down many industries tried to use magical spells in manufacturing...' stated Cranbrook.

'To disastrous effect,' added Williams.

'That is right,' agreed Cranbrook. 'But the dangerous practices were curtailed by the passing of an enabling law making the use of magic subservient to the edicts of the standards committee of the HSE.'

'Yes.'

'And I was looking into flagrant breaches of these standards and guidelines.'

The chief inspector was becoming more intrigued.

'Did you find many?'

'Oh yes,' replied Cranbrook. 'And I was after the chief culprits when I was injured.'

'How did the injury occur?' asked Williams.

'Thaumaturgical feedback loop,' answered Tim, with a sigh. 'A magical process blasted me when it went out of control.'

'Could it have been set up purposely to booby trap you?' asked the policeman, his naturally suspicious nature coming to the fore.

'That's never been sufficiently looked into,' replied the former HSE inspector. 'I received compensation for the injuries but I have not regained the use of my other arm or either of my legs.'

'So not the sort of outcome that you might have been looking for,' remarked Williams.

'No,' agreed Tim. 'What is more I'm pretty sure that the investigation into magical malpractice was closed down after I was injured.'

'But does this relate to the missing people?' asked the big policeman.

'It might,' stated Tim Cranbrook.

He stared at the policeman. The benign expression on the policeman's face had faded and he could now see a malicious grin, like a shark's mouth. The policeman was leaning over towards him. Cranbrook paused, pulling his thoughts together so that he could continue to talk sensibly to the policeman. It was becoming very difficult.

'You'll have to go,' came an officious voice addressing the Chief Inspector. The owner of the voice was a white-clad care assistant who strode into the room.

'He's having a psychotic episode,' explained the doctor who followed the assistant. 'He has been subject to those ever since his accident.'

Peter Whittington walked quietly into the room behind the

doctor.

'Hello Dick,' said Tim, in a small, frightened voice. 'What's happening?'

'You're fine,' replied his friend. 'The inspector was just going.'

Inspector? Tim was confused. Why was a policeman sitting there? Was it really a policeman?

There was something he wanted to tell the man, but what was it?

'Can I speak to the inspector for a few minutes more?' asked Tim, trying hard to shake off the impression that the policeman had changed from a shark into a giant jellyfish with suckers, inappropriately dressed in a blue uniform.

'That would not be wise,' answered the doctor, taking Tim's arm and injecting a large dose of Chlorpromazine mixed with a barbiturate.

'I would be pleased if you would let him speak to me,' remarked Chief Inspector Williams.

'You'll have to come back,' replied the doctor. 'He'll be sleeping this off within minutes.'

Sure enough Tim Cranbrook was already snoring gently.

Peter Whittington helped the white-clad assistant lift Cranbrook onto his bed using a mechanical hoist.

'When would be convenient?' asked Williams.

'Tomorrow, probably,' replied the doctor. 'But it would be best if you did not see him on his own. He is prone to these attacks. So report to the front desk next time you come.'

'I'll return tomorrow morning,' answered Williams, raising his eyebrows slightly. 'Nine a.m.'

'Come in the afternoon,' remarked Whittington. 'He's usually better then.'

'OK,' agreed Williams. 'If the afternoon is better I will come here about two o'clock.'

*

—The number of missing scientists and other professionals has risen to thirty-three. The latest is Professor Fergus G. Smithson from the Bartlett School of Architecture, University College, London. Professor Smithson has not been seen since he delivered a keynote lecture at the International Congress of Architecture in Barcelona.

'It's getting worse,' remarked Detective Superintendent Penny Graves to DCI Williams as they listened to their own spokesperson on the radio. 'How is the investigation going?'

'Nowhere right now,' replied the big policeman, looking around the room at their new headquarters in Bristol.

'What about the guy who telephoned after the TV show?' asked the big man's boss.

'A dead end at the moment,' replied Williams.

'At the moment?'

'The man had a psychotic episode when I was there and they had moved him to a different home when I returned the next day,' answered Williams.

'Did you get any information from him?' asked Graves.

'Only a bit of background about himself,' replied the big man. 'It seems that he worked for the HSE before he was damaged in an industrial accident.'

'The Health and Safety Executive?' queried Graves. 'What did he do with them?'

'He told me that he was investigating magical malpractice and the breaking of safety codes and standards.'

'But he was psychotic?'

'So they said in the home.'

'Did he seem so to you?'

'Not really but his conversation had dried up just as he was coming to the point of his original phone call and he was definitely looking at me in a strange manner. Then the medics came in and sedated him.'

'Have you checked that he really had worked for the HSE?'

'Oh yes,' nodded Williams. 'He had indeed. I enquired immediately. Tim Cranbrook definitely worked at the HSE.'

'It would be interesting to ask again,' remarked Graves. 'Especially if there is some kind of cover-up going on. The people in the home might have purposely shut him up.'

'I did not inform the home that I was visiting when I first went there,' countered Williams. 'So I don't see how they could have known what he was going to tell me or what I was asking him about.'

'Unless he is a special patient who they monitor constantly,' replied Graves.

'True,' agreed Williams. 'And I did go there in full uniform after the medal ceremony we all had to attend.'

'Which might have been a fatal mistake,' replied Graves.

'I do hope not,' replied Williams. 'He seemed a very pleasant man despite his injuries.'

'Let's hope that there is nothing in our suspicions,' remarked Graves. 'And that the man is simply psychotic.'

'Should we talk to the Commissioner about this?' asked Williams. 'He's friendly with Jimmy Scott, the government agent for supernatural affairs.'

'There's nothing to go on yet,' answered Graves. 'But I'll give it thought.'

*

Tim woke up in an ambulance.

They're moving me to the new home, he thought as he looked warily around, moving only his eyes. *The transfer should have been very short so why do I have the feeling that I've been on this journey for some considerable time?*

He drifted back to sleep only to wake up again some time later. It was now dusk outside so he knew that they had definitely been travelling for a few hours. Again he looked around and was able to see out through the darkened window. They were travelling across moorland and he recognised the place from a distant dim memory. This was Dartmoor. The place that he was supposed to be moving to was only a twenty minute journey across the river in Bristol but he must have travelled miles to get to this place. It looked as if he was on his way to Dartmoor prison or, even worse, the new mental hospital housed on the site which dealt with criminally violent patients and the dangerously magically-inflicted insane. The place had already gained the nickname of Bedlam, previously given to the Bethlehem Royal Infirmary in South London.

He did not like that idea at all. Bedlam was a place where people died, they had no experience at dealing with paralysed patients and its reputation was dreadful. Protest groups had been trying to close the place down for several months, Tim had seen reports on TV. The prime minister, Darcy Macaroon, had originally agreed to look into the problems but at the May election Macaroon's party had been ousted and a coalition between the free social democrats and various nationalist and regional organisations had replaced his government. They had promptly shelved any suggestions of closing Bedlam. The coalition appeared to be held together for just one task and was spending all its time passing legislation to split up the UK, not only into the constituent countries but also to politically sever the North of England from the South.

Tim's eyes felt heavy and he could not prevent himself from falling back to sleep again, only waking when his trolley was wheeled in through the main doors of Bedlam to the uriniferous smell of ammonia coupled with cheap antiseptic.

Inside the cacophony from the patients woke him up thoroughly. Patients were hammering on doors, clattering metal containers against tables, kicking pipes.

'What's going on?' one of the paramedics asked an attendant.

'Are the inmates rioting?'

'No,' replied the hardened female warder, a strong middle-aged woman who had hearing aids in both ears and spoke in an overloud screeching tone. 'It's feeding time for the animals. They're always noisy at feeding time.'

*

'Now here's a strange thing,' mused Chief Inspector Williams, studying a text on his smart phone. 'Cranbrook did work at the HSE up until some years ago. But he has not worked there since. He was certainly not there at the time that he told me he had the accident.'

'When did he say he was last working?' asked Jim Rogers, a detective chief inspector who also worked on the same unit.

'Six months ago.'

'Perhaps he is confused about how long he has spent at the home?' suggested Jim.

'He might be confused but that doesn't solve the problem,' countered the big black policeman.

'Why not?'

'Because,' stated Williams a little pedantically. 'According to the text that I just received Tim Cranbrook stopped working at the HSE for one simple reason.'

'Which was?'

'He was dead,' replied Williams bluntly. 'The man died from a heart attack five years ago. So the question is this, who is the chap at the home who is calling himself Tim Cranbrook?'

'Or why have they altered the records at the HSE,' suggested Penny Graves, who was standing at the door and had clearly heard everything. 'Or maybe both questions are pertinent.'

'That's a point,' nodded Williams.

'What was the fellow like at the home?' asked Rogers.

'He's a big chap,' stated Williams. 'Despite his paralysis he is very muscly.'

'Phew!' whistled Rogers looking back towards the large black policeman. 'I've never heard you describe someone as big.'

'This one is big,' repeated Williams. 'Really big. Perhaps four hundred pounds weight.'

'Nearly thirty stone?' queried Rogers. 'Mostly fat I imagine?'

'That's the strange thing,' remarked Williams. 'He still seemed to be in shape despite supposedly being unable to move his legs or his right arm.'

'Was he masquerading?' asked Graves.

'He seemed very genuine,' replied Williams.

'Perhaps he is a very good actor,' suggested Rogers. 'Like yourself.'

'Perhaps,' agreed Williams with a sardonic smile. 'But probably not.'

*

Arthur Burnley stood in the river with a fishing rod in his hand. He had been doing this all day and had not a single bite on his line. This did not worry him at all. He could spend hours in the water on his favourite rivers with not a care in the world. In fact fishing had been cited in all three of his divorces as a form of cruelty and neglect for Arthur would prefer to fish rather than anything in the world and would often go off and leave his spouse for days on end. The poor woman had to deal with the household woes, the children's upbringing, the daily task of managing the finances whilst he did what came naturally: fishing!

My present marriage will probably go the same way, thought the fisherman as he cast his line yet again, not in the least bit concerned about the prospect.

Arthur, often known as Art, did not consider himself to be a cruel man. He usually put the fish back in the water only really keeping them out for display when taking part in a competition or when he had caught a particularly large fish. Monster fish or rarities were his speciality and he did not just fish for them in the

UK. He spent all the money that he could muster on travelling around the world, fishing in outlandish places. Initially his spouse of the moment would go with him, enamoured of the idea of travelling to exotic climes but they soon realised that they would be looking at the sights on their own. Arthur Burnley would be off fishing.

He fondly recalled catching a giant mutant fish, possibly a large goonch, in Nepal. This was a catfish, monstrous in appearance and over seven feet long...the creature had been terrifying the natives and had reputedly dragged several adult men to their death when bathing.

In Russia he had caught the Beluga Sturgeon. Most people when he told them about that remonstrated with him until he explained it was not the whale he was talking about but a very large bony fish. The one he had defeated was over eight metres in length, possibly the largest ever caught, and he had done so by fishing off a very modern boat. He could not have stood in the river Volga to catch that one! Art laughed at the very thought..... the Beluga Sturgeon had one rule: if it could get something in its mouth and swallow it, then that is what it would do....and it had a very big mouth.

'Yo heave ho, Oh, you, Volga, mother river,' Arthur Burnley sang the song of the Volga boatmen out loud as he once more cast his line. 'Mighty stream so deep and wide. Yo heave ho.'

Strange that he had not caught anything in this river yet ... but Arthur Burnley really, really did not mind. It was not the catching of fish that mattered..it was the taking part!

His mind strayed back to the fish he had caught and the other species. No, the Beluga was not a whale but he had caught whales.... he just did not tell people about it. Although illegal and although not fishes, Arthur Burnley had caught cetaceans. Killer whales, narwhal, dolphins, porpoises. Then there were the Sirenia..the manatees and the dugong.

*How that female dugong squealed......*Art laughed at the thought.

Being in cold water above the waist was not everybody's cup of tea but as he stood in the river Art felt snug in his new waders. He had received a personalised advertisement through the post and could not resist buying a pair on the internet. Like his previous waders, Snowbee neoprene, these were state of the art. They completely enveloped his feet and legs, his bottom and waist, and reached up to nipple level then straps criss-crossed over his shoulders....and they were very warm. They were the most comfortable waders he had ever worn, even better than in the advertisement.

The insulation must be terrific, thought the angler. *I've never felt so warm in a pair of waders.*

Chapter 3

Still not a single bite and it was almost time to get out of the flowing river. Arthur Burnley was surprised but he had experienced similarly disappointing days before.

I'm not even supposed to be here, he consoled himself. *So just enjoying the open air is a treat.*

Arthur was a town planner. He enjoyed turning down as many applications as he could. It was his pride and joy to be obstructive, unless there was a suitable backhander as on this occasion. A licence to fish was an expensive luxury and Arthur enjoyed many such permits. His other habit was to delegate any hard work and to pass the blame for mistakes onto his juniors, especially when they were not there to defend themselves. He thought of himself as the teflon man, able to slip out of any difficult situation and able to avoid any hard decisions.

Town planner was a perfect job for a person who like, Arthur, effectively lived a double life. His fishing exploits were well known and in the angling fraternity he was something of a superstar. In the planning department he was in charge of his own section but was almost faceless. Art liked to keep it that way.

The job gave him six weeks holiday a year plus bank holidays. Then you could add study leave, professional leave and sick leave. He was a lucky man because he was almost never sick. You would not have believed that looking at his record. He had fully documented sick leave replete with doctors' letters and medical reports showing that he suffered from back problems brought on by the hard desk work at the council offices. His doctors had even advised him that gentle fishing by standing in deep water was good for his back! What they would have thought of his struggles when catching the the orca he had no idea but that had been when on official vacation and off a different continent so they would never know.

Today it was study leave. He was on a "continuing professional development" course and had duly signed in at the beginning of the day then disappeared for a spot of angling. He would have to leave the river soon so that he could get his certificate at the end of the day. He had already filled in his feedback form indicating that the course organisers were exemplary and the lectures magnificent. Nobody ever noticed his absence just as nobody ever noticed his presence if on the rare occasion he did happen to stay for a lecture or two.

He swung his rod for a final casting and felt the line twitch. Had he caught something at last? His pulses raced. There was a very rare freshwater herring in the lake that this river emptied into. It was known as the vendace and it was only just surviving... it was almost extinct. It was just possible that he might have caught the last one. If he really had caught it, the rarest of the UK freshwater species, he would definitely eat it for breakfast as he would never get another chance. He would not be putting that one back into the lake!

No, it wasn't a bite. It was something jogging his arm. A horrible apparition started to form at the top of the waders.

I've had nothing to eat all day, thought Arthur Burnley. *That must be the reason that I'm starting to hallucinate.*

'No, you're not hallucinating,' said the face on the irregular head that was emerging from the bulge at the top of his new waders. 'I'm really here looking at you.'

'What are you?' screamed Burnley, his heart pounding, fit to burst. 'What are you? Tell me!'

'I am your nemesis,' replied the monstrous creature. 'I am your reward for killing so many innocent creatures.'

'Where did you come from?' asked the absentee from the

CPD conference.

'From your waders,' answered the creature. 'Where else did you think I came from?'

'From my waders?' queried Burnley. 'There was nothing in my waders!'

'Not in your waders. I am your waders...I can change my shape.'

'What do you want from me?' asked the petrified angler. 'I'll give you anything as long as you let me go!'

'It's too late for that,' the monster was smiling. 'I only showed you a face so that I could gloat like you did when you killed the dugong.'

'I never killed a dugong!' shouted the angler, looking around for any help that might come his way.

As usual the stretch of river looked idyllic and, as usual, being a very expensive stretch of river it was completely deserted apart from himself, the present licence holder.

'Yes of course you did,' replied the monster. 'And a whole host of other poor river and sea dwellers. You've illegally fished cetaceans, sirens, cephalopods, endangered reptiles, amphibians, near-extinct fish. You've killed them all.'

'Not true, honestly,' pleaded the fisherman. 'I put many of them back.'

'Only if they were small and insignificant.'

'How do you know this?' queried Arthur Burnley. 'Nobody could know this....and why do you say it is too late to let me go?'

'I can read your mind,' replied the transmogrified waders. 'Every little thought, every misdeed. Your mind is crystal clear and like a big print book!'

'You seem very intelligent for a monster,' replied the town planner, thinking that there must be an angle he could exploit. 'I could be very useful to you. I have considerable influence!'

'I know,' replied the intelligent monster. 'Indeed I do know.

You are a town planner and you abuse your position. You want to offer me permits to fish and other such perks that have illegally come your way. But I am a monster. I have no need for such things. Besides, as I said already, it is too late.'

'Why do you say it is too late?' asked Burnley. 'Why do you keep saying that!'

He was becoming angry with the hallucination. It could not be real. Waders did not talk to you..... they simply kept you warm and dry! This was a mad delusion.

'You're supposed to think that if you notice us at all,' stated the wader monster.

'Think what?' asked Burnley.

'Think that I am a delusionary hallucination,' answered the creature. 'It's part of the effect brought on by the various endorphins and psychomimetic substances we inject into the remaining part of your circulation.'

'Remaining part of my circulation! What are you talking about?' demanded Burnley, speaking in his best and most pompous planner's voice.

'Look down where your legs used to be,' replied the monster, speaking sweetly and gently. 'Then tell me where you think they are.'

Arthur Burnley looked down into the water. He could no longer see a pair of legs. There was just one large trunk-like structure, greenish-yellow, covered in slime and swaying gently in the flow of water.

'My legs! My legs!,' screamed Burnley. 'What have you done to my legs?'

'Calm down, calm down,' soothed the monster. 'Panic spoils the taste of the meat.'

'Taste of the meat?' questioned the town planner, the chronic absentee, the angling superstar.

But he was calming down despite his brain's primitive desire to do the opposite. The drugs secreted by the monster were sedating him very efficiently and he even found himself smiling at the huge maw that was swallowing him.

'Is this how the fishes felt when I caught them?' he asked the monster as he gave in to his fate. 'It's not too bad!'

'No,' replied the creature in annoyance. 'I'll withdraw my tranquillisers!'

The angler died screaming.

*

The trolley bumped along a dull, grey corridor and was then pushed into a dimly lit elevator. The lift moved haltingly up to the fourth floor and the partially paralysed man was wheeled along to a small room with no windows. The walls were padded and there were mirrors on three sides. The door had a peep-hole cut into it.

Two paramedics slid Cranbrook from the trolley onto the bed. The warder had reluctantly retrieved Tim Cranbrook's wheelchair from the ambulance and he now pushed it unceremoniously into a far corner of the room muttering as he did so. Tim thought he said something to the effect that the patient would not be needing the chair and he did not see why the paramedics had made him unload it.

Do they think they can cure me? wondered Tim, still lying completely inert, a skill he had perfected at the nursing home when he did not want the carers to disturb him.

The senior paramedic turned to the warder.

'He's all yours now. Whittington will be along to see him later but this one shouldn't cause you any trouble. He's been heavily sedated.'

'Fine,' replied the warder. 'We're having a case conference about him early tomorrow morning. Perhaps Whittington would like to attend?'

'I'll ask,' replied the paramedic. 'We've got to get back to Bristol now.'

Tim Cranbrook had kept his eyes closed throughout the exchange of conversation. He wanted to know what was going on and he would not learn that if they thought he was listening.

A case conference about me tomorrow? he pondered. *In most hospitals that would be in the patient's benefit but this is not most hospitals. It sounds very sinister. But if Dick is going to attend I'll be OK.*

Breathing slowly and smoothly Tim feigned deep sleep. He did not stir when the warder poked him in the side with her hand.

'You seem deeply asleep,' snarled the warder. 'And even if you're not you soon will be. The neurosurgeons here have a trick or two up their sleeves. Violent beggars like you are no problem at all.'

Violent? What have they been saying about me? wondered Tim. *And a neurosurgeon's solution to my problems does not sound at all encouraging. I was assured that my spinal cord was intact and that surgery would not help so what are they thinking of doing?*

*

The night passed in Bedlam with no further alarms for Cranbrook and he woke at six after sleeping badly. At seven in the morning a large male nurse came in and examined him cursorily but Tim continued to pretend that he was asleep.

The man left the door slightly ajar when he departed and nobody came with food or water.

At eight the case conference started outside his door. Cranbrook had the distinct impression that he was being observed through the mirrors which were presumably one way, designed to allow the people outside to watch him whilst he could not see them.

'This man has been very resistant to treatment,' said a deep voice.

'What have they tried?' asked another, higher-pitched speaker.

'All usual thaumaturgical therapy,' replied the first speaker.

That was what I was told at the nursing home, thought Tim. *They tried to reverse the effects of the magical spell but were unable to do so for some unknown reason.*

'So he is immune to the spells?' asked a third voice.

'Protected against most magic,' agreed the deep voice.

'I doubt if he is protected against my knife,' growled a completely different person, presumably a surgeon.

There was a murmur of laughter that did not ring true to Cranbrook. Why were they laughing at his predicament? Being paralysed was not something to laugh at! And what did they mean when they said he was protected against magic? It was exactly the opposite...the backfire of the magical spells had caused his paralysis and he was not protected at all.

Cranbrook lay still listening to the case conference. He did not like what he was hearing, they appeared to be starving him in preparation for an operation. This was surgery that he had not given consent for and he had not agreed to be moved to the new hospital/prison. Why was this all being done without his consent?

'We need to speak to Whittington about this,' decided the first speaker. 'I'm happy for you to go ahead, Barnard, but Whittington will know whether there are any dangers to you.'

Dangers to the surgeon? wondered Tim. *Do they think that I am an inoculation risk?*

'When will we know?' a deep grunt.

'Around midday.'

'We'll reconvene then,' growled the surgeon. 'But whatever Whittington says I believe that a couple of snips would be the best treatment.'

'Or a quick knock with the chisel,' said the first speaker.

*

'Johnson!' Chief Inspector Williams called out to a smaller man in the incident room of the police station.

'Yes sir,' came the prompt reply. 'How can I help?'

'The missing scientists, sergeant, have you found any connection between them?'

'Not as yet, sir, but I'm working on it.'

'Any new cases?'

'Not since Professor Smithson, sir.'

'Keep me informed,' replied Williams, 'I'm popping out to the HQ of the HSE. I'm going to do a little "on the spot" investigation. I'll be back shortly.'

Daniel Williams walked into the restroom facilities of the police station and a few moments later reappeared in the guise of a repair engineer. Williams enjoyed amateur theatricals and had decided that on this occasion a little subterfuge might just help.

The HSE for the southern part of England was centred at Filton in one of the buildings next to the Ministry of Defence, Abbey Wood, on the outskirts of Bristol. They had very recently moved there as part of the shake-up occurring under the new government. The Liverpool HQ of the HSE was still active but was now serving only the north of the country. If the proposed split did occur all of the quangos, government departments, committees and secretariat would have to be duplicated in the northern and southern regions and multiplied in Scotland, Wales and Northern Ireland. Williams cynically believed that the drive for total independence and the splitting of England was being pushed by the civil service and the politicos with the extra opportunity of employment in mind. Add to that the various European Commission and Parliament appointments and the future for the career politicians looked very rosy indeed.

On the other hand he had been promoted again which had softened his move from London to the South West. Overall he could not complain. His boss, Penny, who he got on with very well, was still based in London but visited the new base in Bristol frequently.

It had still not been worked out exactly where the division between the south and the north would lie but Daniel had seen all the preparatory work and reckoned that the separating border would run diagonally from Gloucester to just below Grimsby. Lincoln, Leicester, Warwick and Gloucester would be in the South. Worcester, Birmingham, Coventry, Nottingham and Grimsby in the North. Bristol was naturally placed to receive departments of Government that had previously been deployed to the north.

A short car journey took Williams out to Abbey Wood, the campus of eighteen buildings which had been purpose-built for the Ministry of Defence in the 1990s. It included multiple offices, lecture and conference facilities and even boasted its own train station.

Williams parked his car some way away from the site and took from his pocket a photo ID card identifying him as an air conditioning repair man.

'Bill Daniels, repairman for the HSE air conditioning,' he said over the entrance speaker system.

'Report to the main desk,' came the reply.

Daniel Williams did not think that his disguise would be sufficient to get him past the security for the main Ministry of Defence offices but the HSE would probably be easier. Sure enough, having displayed his photo ID he was ushered through to the offices. They were in considerable disarray having only recently decamped from Liverpool and secretaries were running backwards and forwards trying to respond to telephone messages.

After explaining that he had to do a routine check on the air conditioning equipment Williams was quickly permitted full run of the department. At eleven a.m. prompt all the staff stopped for coffee in a separate room. Williams had already worked out where the hard copy of staff records were kept so he quickly accessed past files and found the one he wanted. They had told him the truth or at least a semblance of it. Cranbrook was recorded as having died but only after a bad industrial accident involving magic. The heart attack had been brought on by the accident.

Which still left the question: who was the Tim Cranbrook who had contacted the police?

*

A couple of snips?

Tim was no expert on surgery but he was convinced that a back or neck operation would not be a couple of snips and the chisel sounded even worse.

Surely they call a vasectomy a snip? Are they intending to sterilise me? Or even worse: castration!

What could he do about it? What had his friend Dick to do with the surgery? Could it possibly be the same man or were they referring to the Whittington Hospital in Islington, London?

There were too many questions and none of the answers were likely to be good. He did not trust the doctors and he had not asked to be moved to the unit. He did not want to be sterilised and alternatives that involved snips and chisels were even worse.

Perhaps the man was a brain surgeon as the warden had suggested and the snip was to be inside his brain? That would be a lobotomy!

Thinking that he was being paranoid Tim lay back to rest. Obviously lobotomy was ridiculous, he reasoned, but they might indeed try to do a vasectomy on him. Whatever they were planning he wanted none of it. Finally deciding that he had to try to get out of the place Tim, using his one good arm, levered himself off the bed and onto the floor, then painstakingly dragged himself towards his chair.

They had only brought his fold-up wheelchair, not his motor-driven machine, but he could propel himself along with his one good arm. The wheelchair had been adapted so that he was able to go in a straight line pushing with just the one limb.

As he moved past the bed he stopped and quickly rearranged the pillows so that it looked as if he was lying on his side under the covers. Mysteriously there was no alarm raised when he pushed open the door which had remained slightly ajar. Presumably the staff did not think that he was capable of moving.

When he was out of the room he carefully closed the door and wheeled away down the corridor.

At one point he heard raucous laughter coming from a room. The smell of coffee and stale tobacco assaulted his senses and Tim realised that he was passing the staff common room. He glanced at his wristwatch which was still attached to his left forearm. It was just past eleven o'clock.

At the end of the corridor he entered the elevator and pressed the button for the basement, reasoning that there would be no hope of leaving the premises via the front door.

The doors of the lift clattered closed just as one of the staff came out of the common room.

'Hey,' came a cry. 'I want to come in the lift too.'

But Tim was on the move and the apparatus took him so very slowly towards the basement. At every floor Tim thought that the machine would stop and he would be discovered but luck was with him and he reached the lowest level.

The door opened automatically and Tim started to wheel himself out.

Blam!

The door had closed on him, pushing his chair unevenly against the other edge of the portal. The mechanism that should have automatically opened the lift door was clearly faulty and the sliding door kept banging against the right hand wheel of the chair as Tim frantically tried to free himself with his one good arm. Eventually he was able to correct his position on the seat and, by dint of alternately pushing on the left wheel and then pulling on the doorframe, freed himself from the elevator.

Despite the noise, which seemed to Tim to be a terrible racket, nobody had come to investigate. Tim wondered whether to put something in the doorway to prevent the lift going back up but thought better of the plan. It would only draw attention to which floor he was on. So he wheeled himself along the basement corridor, past two people working in a laundry, who gave him not a second glance, and past numerous closed doors, each with a little peep hole at eye level.

At the end of the basement was a fire exit and Tim pushed on it expecting klaxons to sound at any moment. The door swung open easily and Tim was able to see that it had been rigged to allow people in and out. A pile of cigarette ends explained the finding.... the staff were popping out for sly cigarette breaks and needed to be able to get back in easily.

He was now in a courtyard area which led out onto the grounds of the hospital, next to the old Dartmoor prison. The ground was paved in cobbles and he propelled himself over the rough terrain as fast as he dared. He had to get out of view as quickly as possible but it was noon and there was no obvious place to hide.

Drawing on all his courage he wheeled himself out of the courtyard and round towards the back of the hospital. The front gate of the premises would obviously be under observation so it would be better to aim for somewhere at random and maybe, just maybe, he would be able to get over a wall or through a fence or hedge?

He wished that he had made a habit of keeping tools on his wheelchair but then reasoned that they would probably have left them back at the nursing home even if he had done so.

Away from the courtyard a gravelled drive surrounded the building and the going was tough, the wheels digging into the loose surface and leaving a tell-tale groove. Beyond the gravel was an area of grass and a very weary Tim eventually reached that slightly easier surface. Working hard on the wheel of his chair he moved himself over the grass to an area of sparsely planted trees. Thence he was able to move into a truly forested part but could not get very far before he reached a wall fully six feet in height.

He could go no further. There was no way that he could climb over the wall and even if he did manage to do so he would not be able to take the wheelchair. His escape from Bedlam was over.

Chapter 4

'You'll have to find the man,' demanded Penny Graves over the telephone. 'The two stories are not consistent which makes it all the more interesting and moving the man so that you cannot speak to him is very suspicious.'

'You're right,' agreed Chief Inspector Williams. 'But the home won't tell me anything.'

'Speak to Lawrie Pearson,' suggested Graves. 'Here is his number. He'll back you up.'

'Where's he from?' asked Williams.

'He's from the Care Quality Commission. He'll be very interested to know that they have lost somebody they were looking after who had worked for the HSE.'

'Right,' agreed Williams. 'The CQC is likely to scare them more than me. They can close the home down instantly.'

'Exactly!'

*

Tim sat despondently in his chair. Trying to escape in the way that he had done was just silly, he told himself. Just give in to the inevitable.

He was beginning to believe the pessimistic messages in his head and was preparing to wheel himself out of his area of cover when he heard a noise from the wall above him.

A beautiful girl had clambered onto the wall from the other side and was sitting still observing him.

'Poor man,' she remarked looking down at him. 'Confined to a wheelchair and unable to climb the wall....and you used to be so strong.'

'Who or what are you?' asked Tim.

He stared at the girl. She was definitely the most beautiful girl he had seen in a very long time. Tall, slim and lithe, she was sat on the wall cross-legged. Her face was elfin with slightly oval green eyes, a delicate tan and pointed ears.

Is she real? thought Tim.

'I might be just what you want,' the girl spoke enigmatically. 'But on the other hand I might not.'

'That tells me nothing,' countered the semi-paralysed man, speaking in hushed tones. 'Look...I'm in trouble and riddles won't help me now.'

'You'll have to help yourself,' the voice of the apparition was enticingly irritating.

In other circumstances Tim would have found the challenge exciting but right now he just wanted to crawl into a hole in the ground and hide.

'Good idea,' said the girl.

'What's a good idea?' whispered Tim, still staring up at the lovely creature.

'To hide,' replied the girl. 'But you can't do that on your side of the wall. You'll have to come to this side.'

'How do I do that?' asked Tim, trying to ignore the fact that she appeared to have read his thoughts. 'I'm paralysed.'

'You've got one good arm and that still looks strong.'

'Much good that will do me. I can't climb the wall.'

'Follow me,' she instructed him, jumping nimbly to her feet.

I'm listening to an imaginary friend, that's what I'm doing, thought Tim. *They're right. I really am going psychotic.*

'I'm not going anywhere until you tell me what you are,' he announced.

'Isn't it obvious,' she replied petulantly. 'I'm a wood sprite. Sometimes people call me an elf but, pedantically and semantically, the high elves are my cousins.'

Now I know that it's imaginary, thought Tim. *I shall just sit here and wait for the medics to find me. I'm hallucinating all this.*

'No you are not,' the sprite jumped up and down in anger. 'I've told you what I am and you refuse to believe me. You really are infuriating!'

Tim stared at the girl. She was even more beautiful when she was angry, how was that possible?

'Look,' pleaded the apparition. 'You will lose nothing by following me so why not do so?'

Tim pondered the proposition and finally made a decision.

'OK,' he answered. 'I shall follow you, my imaginary friend. But don't think that I really believe in you, because I don't.'

The sprite cheered up immediately and walked nimbly along the top of the wall, even executing a perfect cartwheel like a gymnast on a balance beam. Wheeling the chair one-handed through the undergrowth was in no way as easy but Tim managed to keep up by expending enormous effort. Eventually the wall ended and was replaced by a chain-link fence.

'This is where you can get through,' declared the apparition.

Tim stared at the fence. It looked perfectly intact.

'I don't have any wire clippers,' he concluded. 'I can't climb over with only one hand, I'm far too heavy for you to lift me.'

'Just pull the fence to one side,' she suggested.

'How do I do that?' asked Tim. 'It's attached to the wall.'

'It is attached but the fixings are poor,' stated the sprite.

'This sort of fencing is very strong,' argued Tim.

'But you're even stronger,' trilled the sprite.

'Don't be ridiculous,' Tim countered. 'How can I be strong enough to bend a fence like that?'

'Because you are!' screeched the sprite. 'And I can tell that the people searching for you are getting near so do it now!'

Tim took hold of the fence and pulled at it. Nothing shifted.

*

'He can't have got far,' muttered the female warder. 'He's a big fat paralysed cripple.'

'You underestimate him,' replied Dick Whittington. 'He is stronger than you can possibly imagine.'

'He's a load of blubber,' grunted the warder.

'No he's not,' answered Whittington. 'He looks weak and he does not know his own strength.'

'He's paralysed!' screeched the warder as they followed the trail of the wheelchair over the gravel. 'He can't have got far.'

'He still has more strength in his one arm than you have in your entire body,' replied Whittington.

'I don't believe that for a minute,' argued the butch warder. 'I work out constantly.'

Whittington stopped in his tracks and stared at the warder.

'Tim Cranbrook, as he is being called, is very dangerous,' warned Whittington.

The warder continued to follow the trail.

'Yeah, yeah,' she mumbled. 'I should be so afraid of a paralysed man. So afraid.'

Whittington shook his head and followed her. He was not at all used to people disagreeing with him.

*

'I'll have a word with them and I'm sure they'll cooperate,' replied Lawrie Pearson after listening to Dan Williams' story. 'Wait for fifteen minutes then give the home a ring and speak to the owner.'

'Thanks,' answered the big detective. 'I'll do that.'

Twenty minutes later Williams was armed with the information that Tim Cranbrook had been transferred to Bedlam in Dartmoor. He asked the owner of the home why Cranbrook was being sent to the hospital for the criminally insane.

'He has gone there because it is a safe establishment that can look after his special needs,' the man had replied pompously.

'What special needs did Cranbrook have that prompted a

move to Bedlam?' asked Williams incredulously.

'He has psychotic episodes that lead to violence,' answered the owner.

'Like the one the day before yesterday?' asked Williams.

'Yes, just like that,' agreed the care home owner.

'When he went silent and your team assaulted him just as he was about to talk to me,' added Williams.

'I don't know about that,' sniffed the man. 'That is only your interpretation of the situation.'

*

'Pull on the thing, can't you?' screeched the sprite.

'It won't do any good,' grunted Tim. 'I'll never move the fence.'

'Just try one more time, please,' pleaded his apparition.

Tim checked that the wheelchair brakes were on, took hold of the fence with his one good arm and pitted his strength against the barrier.

Hopeless! he thought to himself but just as he did so there was a rending sound and the chain-link fence came away from the attachments on the wall. Within moments there was a hole large enough for the wheelchair to pass through. With Tim safely on the outside the sprite jumped down from the end of the wall and hastily brushed away the wheelchair markings in the grounds of the prison hospital.

'Now pull it back so that it is not so obvious,' ordered the bossy creature once she was outside again.

Muttering at the indignity of being dictated to by an imaginary friend Tim put some effort into straightening the fence.

'That's fine,' the wood sprite finished examining the damage. 'Now we need to move quickly so that we are out of sight.'

The apparition pointed in the direction that she wanted Cranbrook to steer towards. She followed, rubbing away the tracks behind them and leaving no trace of their passage.. Exactly how the creature managed to clear up their tracks so well, Tim had no idea but the result was near perfect.

They were only just out of view, looking back at the fence from behind some trees, when they heard the warder and the rest of the pursuit party walk by the site of Tim's escape.

'We can't be far behind him now,' the warder's angry voice carried to the pair of them as they hid behind the copse. 'When we catch him I shall manacle him, flog him, put him in a straightjacket and finally flay him.'

'He can move pretty nippily even with just one arm and if his strength were to return....'

'Rubbish,' screamed the warder, looking around wildly and interrupting a voice that Tim recognised as Whittington's. 'He's a blubber monster. I know how to deal with them.'

'We've lost the trail,' stated Whittington.

'We can't have!' screeched the warder. 'He must be near here. We'll keep walking around inside the perimeter.'

The wood sprite had put her hands over her ears when she heard the voices, an action that Tim thought was much like an ostrich burying its head in the sand. The sounds faded away and when they were no longer discernible the sprite spoke to Cranbrook.

'I must take you to a better hiding place,' she stated. 'And then I shall make a decision.'

'What decision do you have to make?' asked Cranbrook.

'Isn't it obvious?' asked the apparition.

'No it's not,' the man in the wheelchair grumpily replied.

'Whether to love you or leave you, cure you or kill you,' laughed the beautiful apparition that called itself a sprite. 'At the moment I would prefer to do the latter.'

*

Jonathan Spenser-Marshall (the third) was a thoroughly unpleasant man. He sat on the borrowed super yacht scowling at the beautiful tanned women who had come with the machine. He was not really interested in the girls at all...he'd taken them with him on the trip because they made him look good and provided good cover but what he was deeply fascinated by was money. Money, money and yet more money. He was a global financier, with a background in law, whose best friend, if he could call him that, was the President of the World Bank. In fact this was the President's yacht and the man had been rather bullied into lending it to Jonathan. Blackmailed would be one way of putting it if one were to examine the transaction closely.

Jonathan Spenser-Marshall (the third) was working on a scheme with factions in Norway and Japan who wanted to bring back commercial whaling. He was also busy raising the finance for a fleet of factory fishing ships which would be working in the fertile currents around the Galapagos Islands in the remote Pacific. Multiple similar schemes utilising loopholes in international law had netted him billions in profit.

At the interim World Economic Forum, an offshoot from Davos but held in the Caribbean, Jonathan had, as usual, met many people from the global political and business elites who were most interested in his ideas. His main method was to look into the laws protecting sites of special scientific interest and find ways of breaking through so that he could exploit whatever the Green lobby were trying to protect. Maps were available showing these sites all over the world and wherever such a site had been set up Spenser-Marshall (the third) knew there was something worth exploiting. The places that had been protected the longest were the ones he liked the best as the resources were usually the most pristine and therefore most easily exploited once he got a toehold into them.

Typical behaviour would be to claim that his exploitation was a science project. If this did not work he might use a third party to poison a water supply, destroy an irrigation system, or perhaps spread a disease or two. Then he would come in using the guise of humanitarian aid..... this trumped nearly all of the laws.

The present interlude was a chance for him to collate the list of contacts and the ideas he had gleaned from the Forum. Some splendidly wicked thoughts were emerging and he really did need some peace and quiet.

He looked over at the bikini-clad beauties and scowled yet again. Picking up his smart phone and computer he retreated into the huge cabin and poured himself a very expensive cocktail.

The yacht was scheduled to stop over a couple of wrecks so that he could go snorkelling but he had no intention of doing so. While the girls were diving he could make some sensitive phone calls to some very dubious contacts.

Chapter 5

The girls had been diving for some time and Jonathan Spenser-Marshall (the third) was beginning to succeed in his telephone and email networking. A method of exploiting rare and non-renewable resources in the Amazon was coming together nicely in his mind and he was the only person who knew all the various technicalities involved. He let out a little snort of pleasure at the the thought that he would, once again, be thwarting the environmental lobby.

Longhaired hippy weirdoes, he thought. *Trying to protect almost dead species at the expense of tax-payers such as myself.*

Not that he actually paid much tax. He had clever accountants preventing that sort of foolish behaviour.

'Mister Jonathan, Mister Jonathan!'

The dratted girls were calling him, disrupting his train of thought. He had told them not to disturb him. It was most distressing and he would just have to ignore them and, when back in harbour, tell the owner of the yacht to withhold some of their pay.

'Come quickly Mister Jonathan. We have found treasure!'

Jonathan Spenser-Marshall (the third) could not resist the temptation to put his head out of the cabin. Treasure was money, and money was his god. They were in international waters and he knew the drill. If they had found treasure on the wreck it would technically be salvage and as the commander of the yacht, albeit temporarily, the treasure would belong to him.

'What have you got, girls?' he asked in as pleasant a voice as he was able to muster.

'Mister Jonathan we have found a chest of gold coins,' smiled the nearest girl.

'Where is it?' he growled.

'It is still in the wreck. Do you want to see it?' asked the girl.

'I don't want to dive today,' replied the financier. 'Bring it up and I'll look at it.'

'Should we photograph the treasure for the marine archaeologists?' asked the girl.

'Just do as I say and bring it up here,' repeated the financier before retreating back into the cabin.

The girl looked disappointed then nodded and leant over the railing of the yacht to talk to one of the girls bobbing about in the water. If Spenser-Marshall (the third) had looked over the side himself he might have noted that none of the girls were actually using a snorkel or any type of breathing aid and that they were staying down in the water for a surprising length of time. But then again he probably would not have noticed anything amiss as he was not an observant or discerning person.

Two of the girls had returned on deck and were hauling on ropes with the help of the girl who had called him from the cabin. Eventually the girl called out for Spenser-Marshall (the third) to come back onto the deck. The financier was just in time to see the girls pull a large wooden box out of the sea and onto the deck. It was the sort of pirate treasure chest that appears in one's dreams. It was draped with seaweed but Spenser-Marshall (the third) could tell that it was of solid wooden construction with a rounded top, the chest was strengthened by brass bands and there was a large ornate lock.

'Clean up the box and bring it into the cabin,' he ordered the girls with no hint of a please or thank you. He then went back inside and poured himself another cocktail.

A few minutes later the girls brought the large chest into the cabin.

Spenser-Marshall (the third) walked round the box, looking at it with interest. As he watched seawater leaking from the chest he thought he could hear a strange singing sound which he took to be vibration set up by the draining fluid.

The lock might prove difficult as might the hinges but I have a few tools in the engine room, he mused.

To his surprise when he tried the lock it opened with ease. The lid also moved freely and he was then staring at gold doubloons! A whole chest full of gold doubloons! It was amazing that the girls could have pulled the chest out of the water since it must have been extremely heavy however not for one moment did Spenser-Marshall (the third) consider that he should have helped them.

The financier knew about gold and he knew about doubloons. Each weighing just under seven grams they were called doubloons, from the Spanish doblón, meaning "double", either because of their value of two ducats or because of the double portrait of Ferdinand and Isabella.

Each coin was worth millions and there looked to be thousands in the chest.

Should I give something to the girls? he wondered this momentarily and then answered his own question out loud.

'No I will not give something to the girls. They're paid handsomely enough to be here and it's not a difficult job. This is all mine.'

Jonathan Spenser-Marshall (the third) grinned as he stretched out his hand to pick one of the coins out of the chest. The coin did not come free from the others around it but this did not perturb the financier. He knew that coins found in submerged wrecks were often stuck together with sediments. He exerted more effort and still the coin would not come free. Intending to get some implements from the engine room Jonathan Spenser-Marshall (the third) attempted to remove his hand from the box. He could not do so, his hand was stuck to the gold coin. Pulling really hard his hand came free leaving two fingers stuck to the coin. In horror he reeled back away from the chest of treasure and stared at his hand.

Had it really happened? There was no sensation of pain and he could not accept the reality of the situation. He looked into the treasure chest and could see no fingers, just the coins so he plunged both his hands in as deep as they could go around the doubloons. He had to know how many coins were there in order that he knew how much the treasure was worth.

This time the mass of coins was coming free but it was still attached to the inside of the box by a thick band of seaweed. Strangely the box was changing shape. Now he could not remove either of his hands from the treasure. The doubloons were losing their shape and merging into a greenish-yellow mass of tentacles that stretched up around his neck and pulled him into the box. The lid snapped shut with an audible clunk

'There are many forms of seduction,' said the creature as it reformed from a monster back into the shape of a beautiful girl.

'And many monstrous human beings,' added the girl who had first called the financier from the cabin.

*

Williams was driving down to Princeton, Dartmoor. Sergeant Johnson was sitting next to him in the unmarked police car and had just turned on the radio to listen to the main news.

- Police in Rome today are looking for six scientist who have mysteriously gone missing from a quantum physics conference. As yet there are no clues to the whereabouts of the six. News is coming in of the simultaneous disappearance of four professors who were taking part in a small seminar in Rio de Janeiro. The disappearances have been linked to the series of more than twenty professional people who have recently vanished from conferences around the world including twelve in the United Kingdom. Two of the missing from Rome and one from Rio are citizens of the UK.

'That puts three more missing professionals firmly in our

jurisdiction,' sighed Johnson. 'I was hoping that it had really stopped.'

'So had I,' agreed Williams. 'And I can guarantee that in less than a minute our phone will ring and our Super will be on the line asking us what we are up to and whether we have heard from Interpol.'

'Which we haven't as yet,' remarked Johnson as his and Williams phones rang together.

'Interpol informing us of the missing Brits,' whispered Johnson.

'And Penny asking us if we are on the case,' replied Williams in like manner.

*

'He's not in the grounds any more,' Whittington had his head up and was sniffing the air.

'How do you know?' asked the female warder.

'Yeah,' agreed her male, white clad sidekick. 'How do you know?'

Whittington sighed. He was tiring of the attitude emanating from the Bedlam staff. He waved his fingers in the air in an arcane gesture.

'What if I said that I can feel it in the force?' he enquired. 'Would that satisfy you?'

'Yeah, I think it would,' nodded both the sidekick and the angry warder.

'Well it's nothing to do with a mysterious force,' replied Whittington, swiping at an imaginary gnat. 'It's logic. We've searched the grounds and he is not in them, they're not huge and he is so big we can't have missed him. Everybody is on alert inside the building and they have not raised the alarm. So he must somehow have eluded us and be already outside the perimeter.'

'Rot,' pronounced the warder. 'He's still in the grounds hiding.'

'I very much doubt it or we would have found him,' countered Whittington. 'I'm beginning to get worried about him. He really isn't stable.'

'You search outside and we'll continue in the grounds,' replied the warder. 'Nobody has ever escaped from here and it's not going to happen now.'

'OK,' agreed Whittington. 'I shall do just that but I shall ring through to you for back-up if I find anything.'

'You won't,' predicted the warder, gruffly.

'But we'll come if you do call,' added the sidekick, enthusiastically.

*

'This way,' demanded the beautiful sprite. 'Follow me.'

'Wait, wait, wait,' answered Tim Cranbrook. 'I'm fed up with being ordered around, shipped across country like a sack of potatoes, discussed in the third person and generally bossed about. Why should I follow you?'

'Because,' answered the lithe beauty, flicking her long hair back off her face in an impatient gesture. 'Despite all my intentions to the opposite, I am your best bet.'

'I just don't get it,' Tim shook his head. 'How can I have ended up in this situation?'

'That's what I intend finding out,' retorted the sprite. 'Before I kill you, of course.'

'Yeah, before you kill me,' sighed Tim. 'That's just a joke, isn't it?'

'Why should it be?' queried the sprite. 'You seem to annoy everyone you are with.'

'I don't try to' replied Tim, honestly.

'It must be a natural talent,' laughed the sprite. 'But you must hurry and follow me.'

'At least tell me your name,' begged Tim.

'Lah Lah,' replied the female apparition. 'Now will you come along?'

Reluctantly Tim propelled his wheelchair one-handedly after the dainty girl with the pointed ears.

Thirty minutes later they were more than two miles from the prison and hospital. They had passed over the immediately adjacent hill and were now down in a valley where a clear stream was flowing.

'This will do,' decided Lah Lah, the sprite.

'What will do?' asked Tim. 'I can't see a hiding place.'

'If you could see it how much use do you think it would be?' asked the sprite.

'Point taken,' agreed Tim.

'It's over there,' gestured the sprite with her long delicate fingers.

Now Tim could just about discern the mouth of a cave.

'It's a limestone cave,' explained the magical forest creature. 'There are plenty of them in Dartmoor.'

'We're going to hide in a cave?'

'Have you got a better idea?' asked the Lah Lah. 'We can't go much further with you in the state you are in.'

'How will hiding in a cave help?' asked Tim.

'If we don't hide they'll find us sooner rather than later,' answered the beautiful creature. 'So let's just do it, shall we?'

With considerable misgivings Tim continued following Lah Lah into the dark opening. Once Tim was safely inside Lah Lah ran lightly towards the exit of the cavern.

'Where are you off to now?' asked Tim Cranbrook.

'I have to obliterate our trail,' clarified the sprite. 'Then I shall return and see if there is any way that I can improve your state of health.'

'Oh,' the reply surprised Tim.

'And if I can't help you maybe I can mend your wheelchair.'

Tim looked critically at the chair which he had given such

a battering over the last hour or more. The sprite was right. The contraption was only just about holding together despite having been made to take heavier patients such as himself. He hauled himself laboriously out of the chair using his one good arm and propped himself up against the wall of the cave, reflecting that it was good luck that it was summertime. The cave was damp and cold with a faint smell of must but the day outside had become hot and the cool of the underground chamber was a welcome relief.

Tim's one useful arm was very tired and sore and he was aching all over. It was a strange aspect of his paralysis that, despite having no muscular control he still had full sensation in his right arm and both legs and they periodically twitched in an involuntary manner . This had prompted the medics to tell him that the paralysis would only be temporary but so far that had not proved to be the case.

Ten minutes later the sprite returned looking a little flustered.

'I was only just in time,' she pronounced breathlessly, crouching down next to him. 'The man you call Dick Whittington is searching for you outside the Bedlam establishment and he had picked up the beginning of your trail.'

'Did he see you?' asked Tim, worried that the game might be over immediately, the sprite could have inadvertently led the man to their hiding place.

'No,' answered the beautiful girl with the pointed ears. 'And I was able to lead him astray, at least for some time.'

She stood up and went back to the entrance.

'Now I shall obscure the cave from outside,' she announced, waving her hands and muttering an incantation.

The exit disappeared from view and the cave became very dark.

'A few fireflies should sort out the light in here,' she murmured, waving her hands again.

The cave was suddenly lit by the glow of myriads of tiny lights, like stars in a clear night sky.

'And now I shall examine you and determine whether I can help,' said the sprite, with a twitch of her delicate nose. 'That's if I decide I want to.'

*

Dame Marianne Foxleigh MA, PhD, D. Sci, Hon. MD, Hon. LLD was feeling rather pleased with herself.

She had been made the equivalent to a knight in the New Years Honour list some six months previously and she had just received another honorary doctorate, this time from the University of Cambridge. All this and she was not yet forty years old.

She stretched her long limbs and patted her hair into place then touched up her lipstick in the mirror. She was meeting a rather yummy man this evening and he looked like a Greek god, just the sort of fellow she liked. She had to look her best.

Chapter 6

'So you really don't know where he is?' asked DCI Williams.

'I've told you once already,' growled the deaf female warder. 'Cranbrook got away. His friend Peter Whittington is out looking for him but it's going to get dark soon so I am expecting Whittington back.'

'How does a paralysed man escape from a secure unit like this?' asked Sergeant Johnson. 'It beggars belief.'

'He's not just any ordinary paralysed man,' grunted the warder. 'He can use his torso and his left arm...'

'Nevertheless it's amazing that he could get away from you,' argued the sergeant.

'Don't labour the point, sergeant,' interrupted the big Chief Inspector. 'I have to agree with the warder on this one. The man is unusually big and fit despite his disabilities.'

The warder looked somewhat mollified and Williams continued.

'But what I don't understand is why he was moved here at all,' Williams paused but there was no reply. 'Why was he moved here from the nursing home?'

'You'll have to ask the doctors the answer to that one,' replied the brusque woman. 'It's not up to me.'

'But you can probably tell me what treatment was being planned for him,' suggested Williams.

'If I wanted to I might,' she agreed. 'But it would be breaking medical confidentiality.'

'Would it really?' nodded Williams. 'I understand. You will let me know if you find Tim Cranbrook?'

'Possibly,' a grunted reply.

'In the meantime I would like to speak to the prison governor,' added the Chief Inspector.

'This is not a prison,' the warder replied haughtily. 'It is a hospital and I am the chief warder of this wing. We have a chief executive officer in charge of the entire establishment.'

'How come you are a warder and not a nurse?' asked the sergeant.

'So that the patients realise that they are not free to leave,' answered the warder. 'It is a secure unit but we pride ourselves on our humane treatment of the inmates.'

'I'm sure you do,' smiled Williams, nor believing a word of it. 'So may we see the Chief Executive? Is he free to see us?'

'The CEO is a woman,' the warder threw the answer back. 'And she's away so I am in charge.'

'Fine, we'll return tomorrow at nine,' stated Williams.

'Fine, you do that,' answered the warder, turning her back on them in dismissal.

*

'That was a particularly good meal,' said the rather yummy man. 'A good choice of restaurant on your part.'

'Thank you,' smiled Marianne Foxleigh.

Dame, no less, she reminded herself. *With loads of degrees … And I've had slightly too much to drink but it's been a great evening.*

'Would you like to go to a club for a last drink?' asked the yummy man, enticingly.

'I think I would,' she couldn't prevent a little giggle as she replied. 'You know you remind me of a good friend. You look much like him.'

'Was he handsome,' asked the yummy man.

'Not as handsome as you,' Foxleigh teasingly replied and felt a little hiccup starting.

That's the champagne, she thought. *It always gives me the giggles and then the hiccups.*

'It's my turn to choose the venue,' the man replied thoughtfully. 'There's great place I know in Soho. It's only just the other side of Oxford Street.'

'Let's be bold and go there,' Foxleigh grinned. 'Do we need a cab?'

'No. We can walk,' replied her date.

'Let's do it then,' she drew in a big breath and felt another hiccup developing. 'Let's walk and you can tell me a bit more about yourself. At the moment all I really know is that you are of Greek origin.'

Much like my other friend, she thought.

'True,' grinned the yummy man. 'I'll tell you more as we perambulate.'

*

'The wheelchair cannot be mended here in the cave,' summarised Lah Lah, the sprite, after examining the chair and the man. 'But you probably can. If you can overcome your own stubborn willpower, of course.'

'I don't understand you, I've never met you before and yet you talk as if you know me,' answered Tim Cranbrook.

He did not feel as if he could be mended. He felt exhausted.

'That's the only reason that I have not killed you,' smiled the beautiful apparition. 'You don't recognise me and your think that you don't know me. So I forgive you.'

'But can you cure me?' asked the gigantic invalid.

'Maybe,' replied the sprite. 'I can certainly try.'

'How?' Tim was mystified.

'A form of magical persuasion,' answered the girl.

As Tim looked at her he began to realise that she was not classically beautiful in the asinine way of some models. The sprite was dynamic and intelligent and that showed in her ever-moving face, the twinkle in her eyes and the movement of her lips. The latter were particularly enticing and he could not stop himself from looking at them as she mouthed words that were incomprehensible to him.

'So when will you start, Lah Lah?' asked Tim.

'Oh,' she answered. 'I've started the process already. Now it is up to you.'

Tim tried to move the fingers of his right hand. Not a flicker. Then his toes. Nothing. He settled back against the damp rock, sighing as he did so.

It was absurd to expect that an imaginary elf or sprite could cure him of his severe disability but he had wanted to believe and he was disappointed. Bitterly disappointed.

*

'I thought that the Whittington guy was called Dick, like the pantomime,' remarked Sergeant Johnson, as they drove away in search of overnight accommodation. 'But she called him Peter.'

'Dick is just his nickname,' grimaced Williams. Sometimes Sid Johnson seemed a bit obtuse.

'So we're looking for accommodation,' continued the sergeant. 'Doesn't look like we'll find any round here. All the B. and B.s have "no vacancy" signs.'

'We'll probably have to pop into Plymouth,' remarked Williams. 'There are plenty of hotels in the city.'

'How far is that?' asked Johnson.

'About twenty-five kilometres straight down the B3212,' replied Williams.

'What's that in miles?' asked the sergeant.

'You do the maths,' growled Williams. 'Multiply by five and divide by eight.'

'Er...' replied the more junior of the two officers, rather hopelessly./

'It's just under sixteen miles,' sighed big Dan Williams.

'That was quick,' smiled Johnson.

'It was easy,' sighed Williams. 'Eights into twenty-five gives you three and a bit. Multiply by five and you get just over fifteen, then add the bits. Rough and ready mathematics.'

'Where will we stay?' asked Johnson, trying to steer his boss away from mental arithmetic onto something he was more comfortable with.

'No idea,' grunted Williams. 'Wait, the sat nav is indicating that there's a hotel really close to us, right here in Princetown. That'll do, if they have room.'

'Let's hope they do,' replied Johnson. 'I put Princeton to Plymouth into my smart phone and it gave me a distance of three thousand, three hundred and fifty-eight miles.'

'That would be Princeton in New Jersey,' sighed Williams.

Oh dear, thought Johnson. *The big man's upset. He usually finds my little jokes amusing but I'm just irritating him tonight.*

*

'As you know I am called Achelous and I have lived in London for the last two years,' remarked the yummy man as they walked through the streets of London. 'I'm into shipping in a big way and I was born in Greece a long, long time ago.'

'It can't have been all that long,' laughed Marianne. 'You look younger than me.'

'It's people like you that keep me young,' answered the Greek god, taking her hand and kissing it.

'You are so gallant!' cried Marianne, boldly. 'Don't stop at my hand.'

'No?' queried the god, swinging her into a dark alleyway and putting his arms around her. 'I am Achelous and I would rather like to eat you.'

'Why don't you?' replied the Dame of Science, amazed at how forward she was being.

As he swallowed her whole she realised that they had meant different things entirely. Despite the supernatural occurrences that had dominated the news over the previous five years, Dame

Marianne Foxleigh MA, PhD, D. Sci, Hon. MD, Hon. LLD in her dying moments still found it hard to believe that the godlike figure she had been spending the evening dating had turned into a giant leech-like creature that was now digesting her in its huge fetid gut.

Chapter 7

'I've come in today especially to meet you,' said the tall lady, most graciously. 'So please make yourselves comfortable. Would either of you like a cup of something.'

She was addressing Dan Williams rather than Sidney Johnson and, to Sid's eyes, Dan appeared rather smitten by the, admittedly good-looking, Bedlam CEO. Detective Sergeant Johnson had to answer on behalf of Dan, agreeing to a cup of tea for himself and coffee for Dan.

'We've conducted an extensive search,' continued the CEO, who had introduced herself as Adelina Aslangal. 'Timothy Cranbrook has definitely escaped from the premises.'

'OK, that's fine,' answered Dan.

'No, wait a minute. It's not fine,' DS Johnson's rebuttal should have been a surprise to DCI Williams but he just looked at Sid with a slightly dazed expression.

'Why not?' asked the CEO, questioning the sergeant rather aggressively.

'This is supposed to be a secure unit, isn't it?' replied the sergeant in like manner. The CEO's charm was certainly not working on him, her looks were too cat-like for Johnson's taste and he preferred short girls.

'As I explained to your superior,' sneered the CEO. 'We believe that Cranbrook had outside help. A paralysed man in a wheelchair, however strong, could not have escaped from here otherwise.'

'What are you doing about it?' asked Johnson.

'We've notified the Plymouth police and they were fascinated to know that you and your superior, Chief Inspector Williams, were on site,' she flashed Dan another dazzling smile. 'They wondered why you were straying on their patch?'

'When will they be arriving?' asked Johnson, choosing to ignore the implied question from the CEO.

'They've been here since yesterday,' replied the CEO, looking down her nose at Johnson. 'They're now outside searching the moor. The patient cannot have got far unless he has been helped by somebody with transport.'

'And nobody thought to telephone us with that news?' asked Johnson. 'Despite the fact that we told the chief warder that we would be staying close by?'

'What good would that have done?' the CEO moved some papers of her desk. 'Now, unless you have any more questions perhaps I can get on with my work.'

'Of course,' agreed Williams, also standing up, still bewitched by the chief executive officer.

Sid Johnson had to lead the chief inspector out of the building, he kept stumbling as if mildly intoxicated. It was not until they were clear of the premises that Daniel Williams shook his head and woke up.

'What happened there?' he asked his assistant.

'You went into a daze looking at the CEO,' replied Johnson.

'I did?' Williams was amazed. 'She's a blonde and I don't even like blondes.'

'You did.'

'Was it something they put in the tea?'

'It didn't affect me,' retorted Johnson. 'And you had coffee. It struck me that the effect on you started before we drank anything.'

'Weird,' Williams was nonplussed.

'Weird indeed, boss,' agreed Johnson. 'But perhaps you have a hidden lust for blondes that you previously weren't aware of?'

'No,' Williams shook his head vigorously. 'It's worse than that.

I can hardly remember a word that was said in there. All I can remember is a burning desire for the CEO. Nothing else.'

'You don't remember me asking her why a secure unit had let an invalid escape?'

'Nope,' Williams shook his head yet again.

'Or that the Plymouth police are here on site looking in the surrounding moorlands?'

Again Williams shook his head and he then brightened.

'But that does give us something to do,' added the chief inspector. 'We shall find the superior officer on the case and see what they have found.'

Johnson groaned. It was a Saturday and he was supposed to be off duty. It looked like a long day ahead. Coupled with that was the fact that his ears were aching. He put his hands to his ears and pulled out a pair of earplugs....he had inadvertently left them in when they got up in the morning. No wonder his ears ached and all the voices had been distorted.

Mind you it really was the only way to cope with Dan Williams' snoring, thought Johnson. *Just our luck that the only space available in the hotel was just one small twin room.*

*

DCI Jim Rogers closed his phone wearily. Another disappearance and he had been asked by Penny Graves to look into it himself. This time the missing person was a resident of Bristol, living in Royal York Crescent, so their unit would have to do the usual common or garden police work as well as the overall co-ordinating role that was their usual remit.

Royal York Crescent was one of the most expensive and prestigious streets in Bristol, a terraced house costing millions.

This is nothing like the terrace house I grew up in, thought Rogers as he looked up at the elegantly curving Georgian building. *This is truly dramatic.*

The building, to Rogers' reckoning, was made up of

about forty houses, each several stories high, and it stood just above a steep hill, looking over the valley of the Avon and the old, gentrified dockland. The view was magnificent but the colonnaded appearance of the houses of the terrace made in themselves a satisfying and spectacular scenic statement on the landscape.

Although Jim had moved with the unit from London his house in Tottenham had not been large. House prices in most London boroughs were high but Tottenham had still not been one of the expensive districts and he had only been able to afford a small place in Bristol in one of the less desirable locations in the south of the city.

Jim eventually found a place to park and then had to walk nearly half a mile back to the crescent.

At least I can park near my house and it is a lot bigger than my old one in London, mused Jim, cheering up a little at the thought.

He strode up to the front door stepping over a bridge-like structure to get to the impressive portal with its arched soffit. Above him he could see the elegant ironwork of a balcony and three or maybe four stories. In the well below on either side he could see the windows of the basement.

Pressing the Regency-style front doorbell he contemplated telling the occupant that electric doorbells did not exist in the Georgian period but thought better of it when the door was finally opened.

'Sorry for the delay,' said a pleasant-looking man who had the appearance of someone in his fifties, greying at the temples, tall and distinguished. 'I was right at the top of the house. You must be Rogers or was it Roberts?'

'Rogers,' replied the detective. 'But you can call me Jim, if you like.'

'OK,' agreed the man. 'I'm Richard Passmore but call me Rick. Come right in and I'll put on the kettle for a cup of tea.'

Jim Rogers was thirsty and the offer was very welcome. He was glad that he had decided not to be petty over the doorbell. It was only because he could not personally afford such a place that he had felt like saying it and if he had been rude it was doubtful that he would have been offered refreshment.

He stepped inside admiring the decor. Tastefully done but not as expensively as he had expected. The place smelt pleasantly of furniture polish.

Passmore led him upstairs to a sitting room that stretched all the way from the front of the house to the back. From the front window he could see for miles.

'Thank you for coming,' smiled Rick. 'I am very worried about Marianne.'

'Is she your daughter, sir?' asked Jim, politely.

'No, no,' responded the elegant man. 'We are just house-mates.'

'House-mates?' Jim could not help but raise his eyebrows.

'We used to be lovers but that finished years ago,' explained Rick. 'We share the mortgage and the house and are the best of friends. But lovers no more, alack and alas.'

Passmore disappeared and returned with two cups of tea.

'Black, please,' Jim requested. 'No sugar.'

'Ah ha,' smiled Rick. 'You're almost the boss but not quite. Perhaps a chief inspector or even a superintendent?'

'Probably never make it now to super,' Jim spoke a little ruefully. 'I'm a detective chief inspector.'

'That's a really high rank,' Rick nodded. 'I was right.'

'How did you know?' asked Jim. 'Or did they tell you my rank when they warned you I was on my way?'

'No rank,' answered Rick. 'Just a message from the Chief Constable saying that Rogers or Roberts was on his way. I think he was a little mixed up.'

'Hardly met him,' explained Jim Rogers, raising his eyebrows at the mention of the chief constable. 'Our unit has only just moved down here and my immediate boss is still up in London.'

Jim Rogers stared at Rick as they both drank tea then he spoke again: 'So how did you know that I was a high rank.'

'Simple,' replied Rick. 'The workers have builder's tea, white with two sugars. Next grade just one sugar. Up a grade: no sugar. Then it's black with no sugar.'

'So what does the top boss have?' asked Rick.

'Next up they opt for herbal tea…usually lemon and ginger or even nettle.'

'And the top man or woman?' asked Jim, with a grin. 'What does the chief constable have?'

'He doesn't drink tea,' answered Rick. 'Just a single malt whisky.'

'And the police commissioner?'

'Back to builder's tea, I'm afraid,' answered the man who shared a house with the missing woman. 'They've got to pretend that they are common folk or they think they will not be voted in next time round.'

*

Chief Inspector Dan Williams and Sergeant Sid Johnson soon found the search party. They had not moved very far from the prison and the so-called "secure" hospital and they could be heard from a goodly distance away. A uniformed inspector was in charge of the team and he nodded acknowledgement when Williams showed his identity card.

'Very good sir,' he remarked. 'Do you want to take over charge?'

'Gracious me no!' exclaimed Williams . 'We just wanted to know how you are getting on.'

'We'll find him eventually,' replied the inspector, relaxing slightly. 'If they've got away by road we'll catch them on the cameras and if they are on foot they won't have got very far.'

'You are sure that there is someone helping him?' asked Williams.

'There must be if he is in a wheelchair,' replied the inspector, speaking a little sharply. 'This terrain is rough.'

'Despite being partially paralysed he is very strong.'

'I thought as much,' retorted the Plymouth inspector. 'Or somebody must be.'

'Why do you say that?' asked Williams.

'We've found the place where he got out with his wheelchair,' replied the uniformed policeman. 'I'll show you if you like.'

They followed the inspector back to the wall and then round to the chain link fence where, when it was pointed out, they could see that the fastenings to the wall had broken and the fencing had been damaged.

*

'Dad!' screamed the girls in unison, running towards him and jumping up into his outstretched arms.

'Hi Milly, hi Molly,' he replied, kissing the twins in turn before putting them back on the floor, a task that was more difficult that would normally be expected as they playfully curled their legs up such that he had to deposit them on their bottoms.

The returning father was then able to give his wife a hug and a kiss before the twins had managed to clamber back up and hug his legs.

'Sally, it's good to be back home,' smiled Kurt Collins, as he sat down on his favourite chair. 'Tell me what you have all been up to here in sunny Plymouth.'

The twins started gabbling together but their mother shushed them,

'We'd prefer to hear what you have been doing, wouldn't we, girls?'

The twins dutifully sat at their father's feet.

'The long story or the short?' asked their dad.

'Long,' they chorussed.

'True or false?'

'False!' their reply was a giggle.

'OK,' agreed Collins. 'Long and fictitious it is, then I'll tell you what really happened.'

The girls, on the carpet, nestled against him and grinned as he started his story.

'A long time ago, in a land called Jamboree, the king asked for an expert in marine biology to be found. Someone who would save the seas from dying due to pollution. They searched high and low but nobody could be found in their own land. So they searched abroad until eventually they found me and persuaded me to follow them back to Jamboree. The path back to the king's land was hard due to obstacles created by the bad bogie man and the bears from the cracks in the pavement. But onwards we....'

'I'll make a cup of tea,' suggested Sally Collins resignedly.

She loved the stories that Kurt wove for the kids but just for once she would have liked to have heard all about the conference with no embellishment. She was worried about the disappearing scientists and wanted to know if anybody that Kurt knew had been affected. Had any of the scientists from the meeting become missing persons?

Chapter 8

'It was seventeen years ago,' said Rick Passmore. 'I was forty and she was half my age but we fell head over heels in love with each other. We bought this place surprisingly cheaply compared with the present prices and did so using a joint mortgage.'

'And now?'

'And now we still live here but with separate lives,' answered Passmore. 'I'm a Reader at the University and she has moved up into the stratosphere.'

'Isn't it a bit awkward living together but not being lovers?' asked Jim Rogers.

'We own the whole house,' explained Passmore. 'We can go days without seeing each other. You have looked at the house from outside, I presume?'

'Certainly sir,' answered Rogers. 'It's big.'

'It's huge!' corrected Passmore. 'We each have our own bedroom, sitting room, bathroom and study....and there are still rooms to spare.'

'But even still...' added Jim.

'We are still good friends,' replied Passmore.

'Fine,' DCI Rogers decided that the point had been covered well enough. 'Now about the disappearance of Marianne Foxleigh....'

'Dame Marianne Foxleigh MA, PhD, D. Sci, Hon. MD, Hon. LLD etcetera etcetera,' the joint house owner had interrupted Jim again.

'Quite,' agreed Rogers. 'Dame Marianne Foxleigh went missing exactly when? And how do you know?'

'Marianne went missing some time on Thursday evening or

night,' replied Passmore. 'You have been briefed on all of this, haven't you?'

'Indeed I have,' explained Rogers. 'But I would like to hear it in your own words.'

'OK,' agreed Passmore. 'No trouble, I can understand that. We might unearth something that was otherwise missed.'

'Exactly,' Rogers nodded as he replied.

'So I shall start with Thursday during the day,' answered Passmore as Rogers took notes. 'On Thursday Marianne received an honorary doctorate from Cambridge. One of a long list of doctorates she has received in the last few years.'

'A long list?'

'She has been collecting doctorates,' explained Passmore in a somewhat disapproving tone.

'You don't approve?'

'It's not up to me to approve or disapprove,' replied the University Reader. 'It's up to the universities concerned.'

'So she received her doctorate in front of everybody at the ceremony. What next?'

'Yes,' Passmore was staring past Rogers into middle distance. 'There must have been several thousand people at the Senate House who witnessed her reception of the honour.'

'Where was she supposed to go next?'

'Rather than come straight back to Bristol she was going to spend the night in London. She had a new date…an assignation.'

'Again you sound as if you did not approve.'

'She did not know much about the person she was meeting. She just described him as being yummy.'

'And then?'

'Then she was due back in Bristol to give a named lecture to the Bristol Medico Chirurgical Society.'

'When was that supposed to take place?'

'Yesterday evening,' answered Passmore. 'They had changed

their evening specifically to suit her.'

'But she didn't do the lecture?'

'No,' replied Passmore. 'I was telephoned by their president who was in a bit of a panic so I went down and gave the lecture in her stead.'

'How were you able to do that?' asked Rogers.

Passmore looked at him in some surprise.

'I thought you knew,' he answered. 'But then you are not from Bristol, are you?'

'I've only been in Bristol a matter of months,' replied Jim. 'So what is it that I'm supposed to know?'

'The research that has made Marianne famous was jointly performed by dear Marianne and myself. In fact all of the original ideas were mine.... so I naturally had no trouble giving the lecture.'

'And yet she has become the professor whilst you are still a reader?'

'True!' replied Rick Passmore. 'And she is a Dame with numerous doctorates.'

'So what did Marianne do that you didn't?' asked Jim.

'She talked the talk and looked beautiful,' replied Rick. 'And it did her no harm at all being female.'

'What did you do wrong?' asked Jim.

'Only one thing,' replied Rick regretfully.

'What was that?' asked the policeman.

'I fell in love with her.'

*

'When we reached Africa we were chased by the younger brother and sister of King Kong,' narrated Kurt, the story developing as he told it.

'What were they called?' asked Molly.

'What were they called?' repeated their father, playing for time as the twin girls stared at him adoringly. 'Their names were Sing

Song and Ding Dong.'

'Were they twins?' asked Molly at the same time as Milly asked which was which.

'They are twins,' he replied. 'The brother is Ding Dong and the sister Sing Song.'

'What happened next?' Molly was asking.

'We ran and ran but had to dive into the sea near the mouth of a river. We started to swim towards an island but were distracted by beautiful sirens sitting on a rock, combing their hair and playing lutes.'

'What colour was their hair?' asked Milly.

'Are they like mermaids?' asked Molly.

'They were all blonde and they were much like mermaids though they had proper legs with fins on them. Now would you like me to sing to you the song the sirens were singing on the rock as I swam past?' Kurt was coming near to the end of his story and he always offered to sing a song.

Sally knew that his singing voice was dreadful but the kids loved to hear him. Then they would laugh and tell him how bad his song had been. Then, at last, Sally would be able to hear the real news from the conference.

'Softly singing sirens
Sighing for a lover
Hear my plea, Hear my plea, hear my plea
Singing for your love enchanted harmony
Come to me, come to me, come to me'

It was hopelessly out of tune but Sally knew he would continue the song to the very end.

'And you will live your life in paradise
Won't need a thing if you just hear us sing
I am sad and weary, waiting for so long
Hear my plea, Hear my plea, Hear my plea
Do not turn away

Hear my siren's song
Come to me, come to me, come to me'

Kurt finished the song, at last, by which time both girls, Milly and Molly, and his lovely wife Sally were all crying with laughter. Kurt pretended that he did not understand why they were laughing.

'And that was it,' he said seriously. 'We didn't swim towards the sirens and they didn't capture us.'

'Why didn't they capture you Daddy?' asked Molly.

'Because we had plugged our ears as soon as we saw them, Molly love,' replied Kurt.

'What did you use to plug your ears?' asked Milly.

'Seaweed, floating seaweed.'

'Yuck!' cried Milly, upset at the idea. 'Seaweed in your ears!'

'How did you know what they were singing if you had seaweed in your ears?' asked Molly, suddenly serious too.

'They had sheet music,' he answered. 'And one piece floated over to me.'

'Why didn't it get all wet and sink?' asked Milly.

'It was laminated with plastic,' answered Kurt. 'Anyway that's what happened and I followed the king's men all the way to Timbuktu land.'

'I thought it was Jamboree land,' stated Molly indignantly, as if she really believed the story.

'They had changed the name whilst the king's men were out searching,' he improvised. 'And when I got there I was able to sort out all their problems. Having done that I came home.'

'Now tell us what really happened at your conference and whether all the delegates were OK,' demanded Sally.

Kurt smiled at his wife.

'Everybody was fine and I helped sort out a minor crisis,' replied Kurt, waving his comment away with a breezy movement of his right arm.

'Which was?' asked Sally, interested. Both Kurt and herself were marine biologists. Kurt's main area of interest was in algal blooms whereas she specialised in a particular type of hermit crab. Sally was only working two days a week now that they had children but when they were older she hoped that she would be able to get back to full time research and teaching.

'Red tides due to dinoflagellates,' explained her husband. 'I was the only expert on algae present at the conference and they hadn't realised that the release of toxins into the air could cause respiratory problems in human beings.'

'They knew about the dangers of ingesting contaminated seafood?' queried Sally.

'They did but one community near the coast had also suffered from a high incident of chest complaints. I think my comments may have been very useful.'

'I expect they were, my love,' Sally patted Kurt on the back and then spoke to the kids. 'Your father has done very well but now we must have something to eat.'

'One more thing,' announced Kurt. 'I'm only back until Monday morning then I must travel up to Bristol for a conference.'

'Another conference?' Sally was taken aback and the twins looked equally dismayed.

The missing persons story, attached to scientific conferences by the media, was worrying her. She had been relieved to see Kurt arrive back safely from the meeting he had just attended and now he was saying that he was going off again.

'I'll only be away until Wednesday,' he held up both hands to stymie any further protest. 'The Prof has decreed that I must go. She phoned me yesterday.'

'How come she didn't know about it before and give you some warning?' asked Sally indignantly. She believed that the professor in charge of the department took liberties by unloading work on the lecturers and senior lecturers employed under her.

'She did know about it but has decided not to go and that I should attend instead,' explained Kurt. 'On the positive side it will give me a chance to show off some of my work and some of yours, if you like.'

'Perhaps we should all go up to Bristol for a couple of days?' suggested Sally.

'I'd like that,' agreed Kurt, brightening up considerably but then becoming serious again. 'Will it be easy to take them out of school at this short notice?'

'No it won't,' admitted Sally. 'It will be very difficult and we may even be fined.'

'So I had better stick to the original arrangement and go on my own,' sighed Kurt.

'If we stuck to the original arrangement it would still be the professor who is going to Bristol,' countered Sally.

'And you promised to build us a treehouse,' said Molly.

'Let's eat and we'll talk about it more over the food,' suggested Kurt. 'And when I come back I'll definitely build a treehouse. Unless you'd prefer a dolls house?'

'A treehouse!' the twins chorussed together. 'We want a treehouse.'

*

Tim Cranbrook was still hidden in the cave with the beautiful sprite, Lah Lah. He had escaped on Friday morning and it was now late afternoon on the Saturday. Lah Lah had brought elfin bread and a couple of bottles of water with her but Tim was beginning to miss real food.

'How much longer do you think we will have to stay cooped up in here?' he asked the apparition.

'Until they stop searching for you and we can find some form of motorised transport to take us away from Dartmoor,' Lah Lah replied.

'How do we know that they are still searching now,' replied Tim. 'It's not as if I was sentenced to Bedlam. They just transferred me for treatment.'

'Is that what you think?' asked the enticingly attractive girl with the pointed ears.

'That's what happened, isn't it?' asked Tim.

'They certainly transferred you from Bristol but the treatment they were proposing would not have been to your benefit.'

'Are you certain of that?'

'All of the inhabitants of Faerie know about Bedlam,' replied the sprite.

'That's the first time that you have mentioned Faerie,' retorted Tim. 'Does it really exist?'

'Of course it does, you've been there!' she responded angrily.

'I have?' queried Tim. 'I don't remember that at all.'

'What do you remember?' she was up close now, staring into Tim's face.

'I was an inspector for the Health and Safety Executive and some months ago I had an accident at a Wellington boot factory,' answered Tim.

'Go on.'

'They were using industrial magic and it backfired damaging my spine and causing me to be paralysed.'

'Really?' Lah Lah did not sound impressed.

'Yes, really,' Tim found he was resenting her disbelief.

'That is what you believe happened?'

'Yes.'

'And did you do anything to precipitate your latest move?'

'I think I telephoned somebody.'

'Could it have been the police?' queried the sprite.

'That's right!' Tim was relieved that he could remember the telephone call. 'I was responding to something that was on television.'

'You were indeed. Do you know what it was?'

'I don't think I do any longer,' Tim was despondent again. 'Do you have any idea?'

'I know that you called them and that a uniformed, high-ranking policeman arrived to speak to you but I don't know exactly what you were going to tell them.'

'How do you know all this?'

'I'm a magical sprite. A wood elf.'

'That's no answer. That wouldn't automatically tell you what was happening to me.'

'No, you're right,' agreed Lah Lah. 'I was in the home myself at the time that the policeman called to speak to you.'

'You were in the home?'

'Indeed,' nodded the sprite. 'I had taken the role, temporarily, of a care assistant.'

'Why were you in the home?'

'I've told you that one already,' stated Lah Lah. 'I was trying to decide whether to love you or leave you, cure you or kill you.'

'And are you going to kill me?' asked Tim.

'I'm sorry to say that I am not,' the sprite spoke with regret, relaxing back onto the stone floor of the cave. 'It wouldn't be fair. What has happened was not your fault.'

'What has happened?' he asked, bewildered.

'Plenty of things,' answered the girl, who was now becoming familiar to Tim, as if due to a form of deja vu, and whose face kept morphing in the flickering light into a familiar pattern..that of a relative or close friend.

'Such as?'

'Such as the fact that you were not in the care home in Bristol for six months.'

'I wasn't?'

'No,' answered Lah Lah. 'You were there for at least the last five years.'

Chapter 9

'You realise that we will have to search this house,' stated Jim Rogers.

'Will you?' asked Rick Passmore. 'Why ever should you need to do that?'

'It's standard procedure with missing persons cases,' explained DCI Rogers. 'We may find clues to her whereabouts.'

'I've no objections to you searching the place but she went missing up in London,' exclaimed Passmore. 'Not down here in Clifton.'

'How do you know that?' asked the detective. 'You haven't explained how you know exactly where and when she disappeared.'

'I don't know exactly where she disappeared but I do know approximately when,' answered the tall, elegant middle-aged man.

'But how?' asked Rogers.

'She lived her life in front of everybody,' explained Rick. 'Recently she has embraced all of the techniques of modern communication. Her entire timetable went onto Facebook and she was constantly twittering to people. She would never have done that sort of thing when I first knew her and it was one of the things that we fell out over.'

'So can you show me her Facebook page?' asked Jim, who was himself quite a fan of the modern media and was the geeky person usually designated to pursue correlations via the huge POIROT networked computer system, which was short for Police Operations Intercommunicating Research Online Tracking and which could follow the positions of people via innumerable digital cameras in all the big cities and crosscheck information from a wide variety of sources.'

Rick leant over and pulled a laptop towards himself and flipped open the lid.

'Here she is on Facebook receiving the doctorate. She posted this immediately after the ceremony. Note that she makes the comment that she is meeting a yummy man for supper in London.'

'Where was she supposed to go after that?'

'She was staying at the Grafton but her bed was not slept in.'

'She could still have been with the yummy man,' answered the policeman.

'And her timetable, also on Facebook, shows that she was due to catch the 10.30 train from Paddington to Bristol Temple Meads yesterday. Again she didn't catch it.'

'How do you have this information so quickly?' asked Jim. 'When people go missing we are not usually involved for several days and it takes a long time to accumulate the knowledge of where a person has and has not been.'

'As soon as I heard that she had not arrived at the dinner before the lecture in Bristol, I telephoned a few of my friends in the police force' explained Rick Passmore.

'Friends?' queried Jim, remembering that the man had mentioned the chief constable of Avon and Somerset.

'Many of the top brass went to the same school as myself,' replied Passmore. 'When Marianne was not at the place she should be I instantly phoned the Commissioner of the Metropolitan police and the local Chief Constable.'

'Then they should have video footage by now,' added Jim Rogers. 'Do we know where she was going to eat on Thursday evening?'

'That was on her Twitter page,' answered Passmore. 'It was at a gourmet pub called the Fox and Glove on Goodge Street.'

'I'll just speak to my boss,' remarked Rogers, thumbing

his mobile phone. 'She may have heard more from the local uniformed boys on the scene.'

For a few moments he spoke quickly into his smart phone and then sat back and waited.

'There should be some footage coming through at any moment,' he told Passmore. 'Then we'll know what this "yummy" man looked like.'

A moment later there was a "ping" on his phone and Rogers was able to see the video. Some very clear frames captured outside the public house showed the missing person, Dame Marianne Foxleigh, walking arm in arm with a tall distinguished-looking middle-aged gentleman. Jim Rogers gasped with surprise.

'What is it?' asked Passmore. 'What have you seen?'

'Unless you have a doppelgänger the yummy man is none other than yourself,' answered Rogers.

'What?'

Rogers could see that Passmore was amazed. The scientist pulled at the phone in order that he could see the screen. There was no doubt that the man Marianne had clinging to her arm looked uncannily like himself.... to all intents and purposes it was himself. He looked at the policeman, utter astonishment written all over his face.

'Is this some kind of joke?' he blustered. 'Because if it is I don't think that it is at all funny.'

'Joke?' countered Rogers, speaking very formally. 'It's no joke at all Doctor Passmore and I am going to have to ask you to accompany me to the police station to help with our enquiries.'

'Wait on a minute,' answered Passmore. 'That does look like me but it definitely isn't.'

'How do you explain the fact that the missing person was seen on the arm of someone who looked exactly like you just hours before she went missing, sir?' asked Jim Rogers. 'And I must caution you that anything you say may be taken down and used in evidence against you. You have the right to remain silent.'

'Whoa!' cried Passmore. 'Now you are arresting me?'

'That's about it if you don't want to come of your own free will.'

'I'll go down to the police station at any time if it helps you to find my friend Marianne,' replied Passmore. 'But first let me tell you where I actually was on Thursday evening.'

'Go ahead,' suggested Jim, taking out his notebook.

'I was in Bristol all evening at a club meeting of the Pink Elephants.'

Jim looked up from his writing.

'Did you say pink elephants?' he enquired.

'That's right,' replied the tall, distinguished man. 'They are a long established dining club which raises money for charity.'

'And they're called the pink elephants?'

'They are indeed,' nodded Passmore. 'I was the after dinner speaker.'

'Can anybody vouch for this?'

'About two hundred members,' answered Passmore. 'Although on my table, the people who saw me there all night would number about nine.'

'Who are these pink elephants?'

'Mostly rather fat men, to be honest,' replied Passmore. 'I was quite out of place.'

'What did you speak about?'

'I want to develop an underwater research laboratory looking for neutrinos.'

'Why underwater?'

'To remove cosmic rays.'

'Can't you do that at night on the opposite side of the planet in a deep mine?'

'The number of deep mines is limited and in the ocean we can reach seven miles down compared with just a couple of miles in the deepest mines.... and the interaction with sea water above the laboratory can be used as part of the experiment.'

'Was Marianne working on similar research?'

'We do tend to write papers together though in truth she stopped doing research several years ago.'

'OK,' nodded Jim. 'For some reason I believe you about the alibi but how do you explain the fact that the fellow has your face?'

'Is it really my face?' asked Passmore. 'I would say that the man is better looking than I am and he is certainly younger.'

Jim stared at the video and the still frames for a while.

'You are right. But what is the explanation?'

'In this age of the supernatural,' answered the research scientist. 'I am obliged to answer with just one word. A word that is rather dirty to scientists and, up until a few years ago I would never have thought that any scientist would use it to explain anything.'

'Which is?' asked Jim.

'Magic, of course,' answered Passmore. 'The fellow she was dating used some sort of spell to mask his actual appearance and to roughly copy my features.'

'It's not a rough copy. It's a very good one.'

'Nevertheless a copy is what it is,' replied Passmore. 'And if Marianne was dating somebody who could use such powerful magic I reckon that we are all out of our depth.'

'You're right,' agreed Jim. 'I don't like this development at all. Not one little bit.'

Jim Rogers telephoned a couple of people from the Pink Elephant's club to check on Rick Passmore's alibi. There was no doubting that he was definitely in Bristol when the doppelgänger had been dating Marianne Foxleigh in London.

'And I certainly do not have a twin brother,' Passmore had added in answer to the unspoken question.

'OK,' agreed Rogers. 'Magic becomes the most likely explanation. I understand that in Faerie they can imitate almost anybody so perhaps they can do that here now that the worlds have collided.'

'Do you have a branch of the police force set up to deal with magic?' asked Passmore. 'If, as in the old legends, folk from Faerie are abducting people then you need a section dealing with it.'

'Not really Rick,' replied the detective. 'Though we have set up special iron holding cells that negate the magical effects.'

'What about Jimmy Scott?' asked Passmore, noticing that they were back on first name terms again now that Jim Rogers believed his alibi.

'The other famous Jimmy?' Rogers raised an eyebrow. 'He's a Bristol resident isn't he and we have discussed talking to him.'

'I could talk to him informally,' suggested the tall Reader from the University.

'You know him?'

'Bristol is not all that large a place and he used to be my electrician.'

'OK,' agreed Rogers. 'You phone him while I contact my boss. She'll need to know what we are doing and warn the others on the case that we suspect magical interference.'

Rick Passmore could tell that Rogers did not like to use the word magic on its own. This was commonplace....despite the supernatural cataclysms many educated people still did not like to refer to the causation of events as being due to magic. The rule of science and technology had become so great in people's minds that to admit that something was outside their knowledge was very difficult. Something similar had occurred at the end of the Nineteenth Century when it was thought that all of science was understood...only to have their complacency blasted away by the discovery of X-rays by Roentgen and radioactivity by the Curies followed not long afterwards by the development of Quantum

Mechanics, describing the subatomic world, and Relativity the cosmic level of reality.

'It might make it easier if you use the words thaumaturgical science,' urged Passmore. 'I'm happy to just call it magic and accept that it is a natural phenomenon which I don't yet understand but I can appreciate your reluctance to use the word magic. It reeks of fakery and flim-flam.'

Jim Rogers looked at Passmore contemplatively. The man was right. Why hadn't they got a special unit set up to deal with magic? It was clearly important and they did everything concerned with it in an ad hoc way. It was time that magic was sorted out and with regard to policing they would need a new way of looking at problems.

Penny Graves answered her phone immediately and Jim told her the developments.

'I'll telephone the other teams working on the disappearances,' she replied. 'Will you phone Dan Williams?'

Rogers agreed to contact his fellow chief inspector.

'And I concur with the idea of enlisting Jimmy Scott's help,' she added then cut the phone call.

Rogers looked over to Passmore who was busily in conversation on his own telephone landline. Jim decided that he had better speak to Dan Williams and tried his mobile immediately. He could not get through directly so he left a message on his voicemail.

Passmore finished his conversation and told Rogers that Scott was away but he had spoken to Scott's son who had very sensibly suggested they enlist the help of the ambassador from Faerie. He had given Rick the number but there was, again, no immediate reply.

'OK,' proposed Jim Rogers. 'I'll take it from here. This could take some time and I have used up enough of yours already.'

'It's not a problem,' replied Passmore. 'I just want to help as much as I can.'

'Do you have any other suggestions, however unlikely?' asked Rogers, slipping back into his usual practical policing role.

'Just that rivers and the sea may be involved,' replied Passmore. 'Some of the missing scientists have been marine biologists and our work involved the sea.'

'But a lot of them were not related to water,' replied Rogers. 'But I'll give it thought.'

Chapter 10

'Do you believe that the police have gone?' asked Tim Cranbrook after another fitful night's sleep and a day spent just eating elfin bread.

He was developing a painful cramp in both his legs and in his right arm. This was something that had occurred before but only rarely and in the nursing home Dick Whittington would help him into a hot bath and the cramps would wear off.

'Maybe,' replied Lah Lah, the mysterious sprite.

'Because I'm getting rather miserable down here,' continued Tim. 'I'm cramping up.'

'That's good news,' replied the sprite. 'It means your muscles are beginning to work.'

'Not if you're the one with the cramp,' grunted Tim as he moved his big heavy body using his one, admittedly very strong, arm.

Lah Lah was stood against the concealed entrance of the cave listening to the outside world.

'I'm pretty sure the police have gone but I think that your pal Whittington is out there on his own.'

'Really?' asked Tim. 'He's always been very helpful towards me. Perhaps in the absence of the warder and the police he can help us.'

'I very much doubt that,' answered the sprite. 'He is very persuasive when he tries to be but I'm not so sure that the persuasion is there to help you.'

'Come now,' replied Tim. 'The only reason that I did not want to give myself up to him was that he was accompanied by the warder and her cronies. He probably didn't know what they wanted to do to me.'

'And what did you think that they wanted to do?' asked Lah Lah.

'I think they wanted to sterilise me!' the big paralysed man replied indignantly. 'They were talking about a couple of snips.'

'And that prompted you to break out?'

'Well, yes,' replied Tim, slightly confused. 'Don't you think it should have done?'

'Of course,' she replied. 'But I believe it was your subconscious that told you to get out as quickly as possible, not a truly conscious decision.'

'Perhaps, whatever,' replied Tim.

'It's not whatever,' the sprite was angry. 'You are so big and stupid sometimes. They didn't want to sterilise you!'

'So what did they want to do?'

'They're a penal hospital for the criminally insane and the surgeons are neurosurgeons.'

'Neurosurgeons are good guys,' protested Tim.

'Not the ones who want to do a frontal lobotomy on you just so that they can control you!' screamed the sprite.

Tim sank back against the stone. It was true that he had considered that they were discussing brain surgery but it had seemed such a remote possibility that he had dismissed it. Perhaps his subconscious had not ruled it out? That would explain why he had thought that early escape was essential.

'Late escape would not have been possible,' replied the sprite, reading his mind again.

A voice came floating over the wind. It was the dulcet tones of Peter Whittington, otherwise known as Dick and the only friend he could remember in the nursing home.

'Hello Tim,' he was saying very pleasantly. 'I know that the move from Bristol frightened you but there is no reason to be alarmed. We are only trying to help you.'

Tim sat still, ignoring Dick's seductive voice and Whittington changed his tack.

'Now I am speaking directly to the person who is helping Tim,' Dick started.

'I don't want to hear. I don't want to hear. I don't want to hear,' Lah Lah sat with her hands over her ears but the voice of Peter Whittington was filtering through the makeshift barrier of frail sprite flesh.

'The best way to help Tim is to come out into the open and give yourselves up. I repeat come out into the open and give yourselves up.'

Suddenly, to Tim's utmost astonishment the sprite leapt up and tore apart the barrier, both physical and magical, that she had put across the entrance. What was she doing after all the effort she had gone to in order to hide them? Why was she doing it when she had said that Dick was not his friend?

'Ahhh,' sighed Dick. 'A sprite or wood elf. I should have known. They're renowned for their ability to hide their tracks. Come to me little elf.'

The sprite walked timidly out of the cave and sat, at Dick's bidding, by his feet.

'Now Tim,' Dick was addressing him and the fear of betrayal disappeared from the big crippled man's mind, this was his friend helping him. 'Bring yourself out here, if you can, that's a good fellow.'

Tim Cranbrook dragged himself out of the cavern, painfully moving over the broken terrain.

'My, my. You are in a bad way and your wheelchair is broken,' declared Dick, after peering into the cave. 'Never mind. We will call for help and they will bring another one.'

He stopped for a moment and spoke on his cellphone.

'They're on their way,' he announced. 'Now sprite, you don't want anybody to see you, do you?'

She shook her head.

'Quite right,' continued Whittington. 'So it would be better for everybody if you went back into the cave.'

The sprite was fighting with herself and was reluctant to move.

'Now!' screamed Whittington. 'Before the rescue party arrives.'

The sprite was unable to disobey and, leaping to her feet, scurried back into the cave.

Once she was safely inside Whittington made Tim look at her.

'She's not what you thought she was, is she?' he stated.

Tim looked in and at first could see the pretty girl staring at him and mouthing the words "Help me, Help me," over and over again. Then she morphed into a leech-like shape with a huge mouth which was slobbering fetid saliva.

'That's her real shape,' remarked Dick.

The creature now appeared to be telling Tim not to take a bath. It definitely was saying it!

'Don't take a bath. Whatever you do don't allow Dick to get you into a bath. Don't take a bath!'

Whittington took a small round object from his pocket and threw it at the opening of the cavern. There was a muffled explosion and the cave collapsed on the ugly creature.

'That's shut it up. Don't worry about it,' Dick told Tim as he jumped with horror. 'That's the best thing to do with creatures like that.'

'What was it?' asked Cranbrook.

'It was a mind leech,' replied Whittington. 'They are parasites that make you believe that black is white and vice versa. They are all evil. I've seen them before.'

Tim was not sure whether to believe Dick or not. First he had said she was a sprite and now he said she was an evil mind leech. How could she have been both? Part of his brain was programming him for fight or flight and the other part was docilely lying down to receive whatever treatment they sent his way. After a feeble struggle the docile part won as he had no convincing way of either running or fighting. He could hear the whup, whup ,whup of an approaching helicopter and he was not surprised when they landed only a few yards away from him.

'Don't worry,' ordered Dick. 'You'll be fine. I'm coming with you this time.'

A good thing or a bad thing? Tim could not decide but he gave in to the inevitable as a team of men came and placed him on a stretcher and carted him off into the air ambulance.

*

'I understand that you have discovered the whereabouts of Tim Cranbrook,' stated Chief Inspector Williams as he stood with Sergeant Johnson, trying to persuade the chief warder to let him into the hospital block. It was early on the Monday morning and he was not feeling in the best of moods. It had been worsened by a voicemail from Jim Rogers saying that he suspected magic was involved in the series of missing professionals.

Teaching him to suck eggs! Why the heck did Rogers think that I'm chasing Tim Cranbrook for more information?

It was obvious that magic was involved in Cranbrook's case so he was not at all surprised that it might be involved in the missing professionals investigation. Dan Williams longed for the time when the criminals had been simple thieves and muggers. Or even when they had surgeons alter their appearance so they could take the role of the Vice President...that had been simpler than dealing with this lot. The whole of Sunday until the hunt was called off they had been out on the moors with the local police.

'I don't believe so,' replied the belligerent woman after a long pause, cutting through Williams' reminiscence. 'No, I don't believe that we do know where Cranbrook is.'

'Well I do,' stated Williams. 'And unless you stand to one side and let us enter the building I shall arrest you for impeding law enforcement and obstructing the work of the police.'

'We'll see about this,' muttered the awkward woman but she stood aside very reluctantly and the two policemen strode down the corridor to the elevator.

At the fourth floor they went straight to the room that they had been told was occupied by the big paralysed man. They had obtained the information from one of the air ambulance paramedics who they had met in the hotel bar late the night before. To their surprise and disappointment the room was empty.

'What do we do now?' asked Sid Johnson. 'He is one of our only leads.'

'If you are looking for the patient called Tim Cranbrook,' said a querulous female voice. 'He is on his way to the surgery suite.'

'Which way is that?' asked Williams.

'Level two in the next block along,' stated the small woman who was dressed in a shapeless smock and was wielding a mop and bucket. 'I'll be over there cleaning soon enough.'

'Thanks,' cried both policemen together.

'Take the stairs, they're quicker,' instructed the wavering voice.

'Thanks again,' shouted Williams as they bounded carelessly down the stairs, three at a time. Across the courtyard and up into the next building they raced. Management on all levels! No signs of an operating theatre.

'It must have been the next block in the opposite direction,' suggested Sid Johnson.

'Unless she was purposely trying to mislead us,' growled the big policeman.

It *was* the next block that the cleaner had meant for the signs indicated that the operating theatres and recovery rooms were on level two, X-ray was on level one and Intensive Care on four.

They ran up the stairs to level two, Johnson trailing behind Williams and gasping for breath. There was no sign of the large invalid within the theatres except for a note written with removable felt tip on a white board. It stated: *Tim Cranbrook 9.30 Frontal Lobotomy.*

Williams looked at his watch. It was twenty past nine so Cranbrook was not expected to be operated on for ten more minutes. Perhaps they were preparing him for anaesthetic?

They looked wildly around for the man but could see no sign.

'Of course he might be having X-rays first,' came the querulous voice.

The cleaner had caught up with them!

'They often have CT scans of the head before a neurosurgical procedure,' she said in a worldly-wise manner, her head cocked to one side like a starving sparrow watching an early worm. 'Or if they are very interested they might even do an MRI scan.'

They ran down to level one and were stopped at the door of the MRI suite. Sure enough through a small window that appeared to be made of safety glass they could see the big man being taken into the MRI machine.

'We have to question that man,' stated Williams.

'The patient?' asked the male radiographer, nonchalantly looking in the direction of Cranbrook.

'Yes, the patient!' shouted Williams.

'Too late,' said the radiographer languidly. 'They've started the scan.'

'But I don't want him to be harmed. I need to speak to him,' muttered Williams.

'Don't get your knickers in a twist,' replied the radiographer. 'It's only a large magnet and some radio waves. It won't harm him at all.'

'So I can go in and speak to him as soon as the scan finishes?' asked Williams, ignorant of the exact workings of an MRI machine although he was aware of its value in showing sectional images of the body.

'Not unless you have already been screened to remove all

metal from around your person,' remarked the radiographer. 'If you do have metal on you it could pull out of your clothing and act like a missile, or heat up and burn you.'

'I'll stay outside and wait,' replied Williams resignedly. 'But don't let him get away from here without me speaking to him.'

'How long does the scan take?' asked Johnson.

'Between half an hour and an hour,' sighed the radiographer. 'Now if you don't mind I have work to do.'

'So he will be late for the neurosurgeons,' stated Williams.

'They're the ones who asked for the scans,' answered the radiographer, shrugging his shoulders. 'Now go away while I work.'

He returned to the control desk to help another radiographer who had been processing the sequences on the machine.

Williams and Johnson sat outside to wait.

*

Kurt took the train from Plymouth to Bristol Temple Meads. As always he felt a little thrill as he positioned himself in the coach such that he could look out to sea where the South Devon Main Line ran along the sea wall. The rail line shared this with a coastal path and Kurt always enjoyed imagining himself hiking along the route on a bright summer's day.

This Monday it was presently very misty but he knew that this was only a sea mist and would clear later as the sun became hotter. The local fishermen usually called it fog but as he had stood on the platform waiting for the train in Plymouth he had heard an old lady say that the weather was larry, which presumably referred to the mist. In other parts of the country it might have been described as a sea fret.

His pulled his straying mind back to the task ahead. His professor had sent him the Power Point projection she had intended using but it needed adaptation so he brought out his laptop and got to work.

Half an hour later he had altered the material to his liking and had even included slides of his own work and Sally's. He sat back to read a fantasy novel.

Not that it is easy to define which is fantasy and which is real, he thought to himself. Just five years ago there had been the supernatural intervention at Stonehenge as two or maybe three realities clashed. Worlds colliding was the term that was often used but this was more than just planetary collision. There had been catastrophic changes to the universe as universal constants had shifted. The physicists blamed it on the collision of branes in a multiverse. Kurt was inclined to accept the common understanding that Parsifal X, a powerful entity from a parallel world, had engendered the collision, though the energy and force he must have wielded to do that beggared belief.

The train pulled into Temple Meads station. The old buildings from the first station were still standing but the present station had been further developed in 1870, 1930 and four years previously. Kurt quickly detoured through the more open part of the old building to pay homage to the great engineer, Isambard Kingdom Brunel, who had opened, in 1840, Bristol's first railway station as the western terminus of the Great Western Railway from London, Paddington.

Outside the station buildings he hopped into a taxi and asked the driver to take him to Bristol Zoo.

'You after looking at the lions, today?' asked the man.

Kurt explained that he was talking at a meeting.

'Ah, reet,' the driver nodded. 'Then you'll be wanting the entrance down the side not the one at the front. Mind, it's worth seeing the lions if you get a chance. I understand that they have some new cubs.'

The journey was relatively short as Kurt rehearsed his lecture in his head and he immediately recognised some of the delegates as they also arrived at the venue.

When he announced his name at reception he was greeted warmly. Organisers were always particularly pleased when speakers arrived, it was one more worry they could discard. Kurt knew this and never liked to do the trick that some speakers practised of arriving just before they were speaking and then waltzing straight off again. In his own case the meeting organisers were more than usually delighted as his professor in Plymouth had warned them that she could not speak and had said that it was likely Kurt Collins could do the lecture in her stead. She had also mentioned that she could not be absolutely sure as Kurt was away giving a talk elsewhere. The latter had been a bit of an exaggeration as Kurt had been on a panel but had not actually given a lecture but he understood why she had said it.

Then, of course, there was the problem of disappearing professionals. The meeting organisers might well have been worried that the widespread news of lecturers who went missing from conferences might put off the speakers from turning up for their talk.

Anyway...he was here in Bristol with his powerpoint lecture and would be ready to present on time to whoever attended...and there was no doubting the heartfelt relief on the organisers' faces.

*

Peter Mingan, the werewolf, was the acting ambassador for the Faerie reality. He was based in London and had agreed to meet Superintendent Penny Graves later on the Monday. In the meantime Jim Rogers was sat at his computer in Bristol trying to see whether the suggestion of a maritime connection would hold water, a pun that had already commended itself to him for comment if he did find that it was the case. All of the occupations of the people worldwide who came into category of missing professionals whose absence had been noted from conferences had been entered onto the POIROT program. Searching by occupation did show that at least a third were involved in some kind of water-based occupation. This was far higher than should have been the case purely by chance but did leave two-thirds who were not connected in that way. He sat fiddling with various combinations of ideas based on addresses plus occupation. This did not help much as the vast majority of cities were either next to the coast or on rivers and a random selection of missing persons gave almost exactly the same result: they were nearly all connected to rivers or seas in some way.

Jim sat back praying for inspiration.

*

The morning session had finished and Kurt Collins' lecture had been well received. The chairman had hinted that it was better than the last lecture given by Kurt's professor but Kurt had played that down and had acknowledged that the presentation was not his own and he had simply adapted it slightly. It was lunchtime and he took a quick bite to eat...he had nearly an hour in which to look round the zoo and he did intend seeing the baby lion cubs if they were on display. He was also particularly interested in the okapi. This was a strange animal from the Congo in Central Africa. Kurt had only seen one before but Bristol Zoo had a whole family.

The lion cubs were fine but the okapis were better. They looked as if they had been designed by a committee... one that could not make a definitive decision so had thrown in anything they thought of. The body shape was reminiscent of a giraffe, their closest relative, although the neck was much shorter. Then there were the legs: horizontal black and white stripes which made the animal look as if they had borrowed their limbs from a zebra. The tongue of the okapi was something to be admired also. It was hugely long and he watched fascinated as one animal cleaned its ears both inside and out.

'It's a fascinating animal isn't it?' said a voice in dulcet tones.

Kurt turned in surprise as he had not heard anybody walking

towards him. One of the delegates from the conference, a beautiful young lady, was standing next to him. She was much like Sally but just a bit younger and quite a stunner.

'Your lecture was excellent,' she remarked. 'I wondered if you would like to take me through a few points again.'

She said this in a very seductive voice and Kurt had no doubt that something other than his lecturing skills was on her mind. A picture of his two young daughters sprang into his head and he replied instantly.

'You'll have to e-mail,' he said this as he gave her a card. 'I've got to get back to the afternoon session.'

The expression on her face was extraordinary. As if her offers have never been refused before.

I'll probably regret that in years to come, thought Kurt. *She really was the most exquisite female I have ever seen.*

He almost walked back to her but Milly and Molly were telling him not to do so.

*

Dan Williams glanced at his watch yet again. They had been waiting for well over an hour and there was no sign of the patient coming out of the MRI scanner.

'They're taking their time scanning Cranbrook,' he muttered, rising to his feet and staring through the windows.

There was no sign of anybody in the suite.

'There must be another exit,' growled Williams. 'They've managed to fool us.'

They ran round to the other side of the MRI suite and found that the supposition was correct. There were double doors leading into the scanner room that had not been visible from the other side.

In the distance they could just see the indifferent radiographer disappearing into a staff room so they ran after him.

'Where have they taken Cranbrook?' asked Johnson, taking

hold of the man's arm.

'Easy,' smoothed the radiographer. 'What's all the fuss?'

'We wanted to speak to Cranbrook as soon as he came out of the machine,' Williams reminded him. 'Don't you remember?'

'Oh yeah, so you did,' agreed the radiographer in an unconcerned manner. 'I expect he has been taken to operating theatre number 3 but I don't really know.'

'That's on level two? Right?' demanded Williams.

'Sure,' agreed the radiographer. 'One floor up.'

'How long ago did he leave?'

'About ten minutes. Why are you so worried?'

'We need to speak to him when he is in a compos mentis state. If he isn't conscious when we get there you may well need a lawyer as I will be arresting you for obstructing police work.'

Williams and Johnson ran up to level two and into the operating theatres. Cranbrook was lying on a table in the anaesthetic preparation room with two surgeons, an anaesthetist, three nurses and Peter Whittington holding him down. Whittington was persuading the big, paralysed man to lie still but he did not want to oblige. Then he suddenly went limp. They had managed to get an injection into his arm.

'What have you done to him?' asked Williams, as he looked round wildly at the personnel in the room, trying to work out who was who.

'I've given him Midazolam,' replied the man who was obviously the anaesthetist. 'But who are you to question me.'

'I am a senior police officer,' retorted Williams. 'By the name of Chief Inspector Williams and this is Sergeant Johnson. You are all under arrest for obstructing the law.'

'Rubbish,' cried one of the surgeons. 'I'm in charge here. You are not in sterile clothing so get out of my operating suite.'

'We need to talk to the man you have just anaesthetised,' countered Williams. 'And I have made that clear on several occasions and everyone here has been preventing us from doing so.'

'Get out,' shouted the surgeon again, waving surgical instruments in the air.

'No I won't,' replied Williams. 'And if you don't put that scalpel down I shall call for back-up and I really will have you put in the slammer.'

'Ignore this man and we will get on with the procedure,' suggested the other surgeon. 'I have a very simple technique with a hammer and chisel and we'll have it all done in moments.'

'No you don't,' cried Williams and he stepped forward with Johnson to prevent the surgeons from attacking Cranbrook.

'I shall get help,' whispered Whittington to the anaesthetist as he sidled out of the suite before the policemen could stop him.

Within minutes the smooth CEO of the hospital was entering the suite with a very angry look on her face.

'Now, now Inspector Williams,' she murmured. 'I thought that you and I were friends?'

Daniel Williams face went blank and he then began to smile benignly at the CEO. The woman continued to speak calmly to the policemen.

'I would like you to leave the suite please and go downstairs and out of the hospital,' she had clearly won over Williams and she turned to Johnson. 'And the same for you Sergeant Johnson.... and don't come back!'

The last part was more of a snarl but Dan Williams did not seem to notice this. Johnson stood in two minds and was wavering on the side of leaving when the little cleaner lady came up next to him.

'Put your fingers in your ears,' she said. 'It's the best way to stop her persuasion from working.'

'What about earplugs?' asked Sergeant Johnson, taking some out of his pocket.

'Try them,' suggested the cleaner.

Johnson obliged and then, with no protest from his boss, he put some in Williams ears. Meantime the CEO was still shooing them out of the room.

'Stop that at once!' ordered DCI Williams, with speed positioning himself, once more, between the surgeons and the patient. 'We are staying here until the anaesthetic wears off and I expressly forbid you from operating on the patient.'

The CEO started shouting at Williams as loudly as she could but the big policeman steadfastly ignored her. Eventually she gave up and left the room.

The surgeons walked off to the changing room in a huff and the policemen sat down beside Williams and waited.

*

The Bristol meeting at the zoological gardens finished at four-thirty, an hour and thirty minutes earlier than expected due to the absence of two lecturers. Kurt realised that he could have travelled back to Plymouth and then returned in the morning but he was already booked into a budget-priced hotel just a half mile away from the zoo and it would cost much more to cancel and then return, so he resigned himself to staying the night.

He was absorbed in thought as he walked away from the zoo, thinking about the reason that the speakers had cancelled and wondering whether it was due to the disappearances. Were they concerned that they might be the next target? He certainly did know rumours about some of his colleagues who had refused invitations. Had they actually disappeared themselves?

As he wandered along he did not notice somebody following him, a person who was working hard to keep out of sight.

Chapter 11

'Pulpo en el carnaval,' Jean-Michel Starr, the celebrity chef smiled at the camera. 'This is not a dish that can be prepared in a hurry. You should start your preparations two weeks in advance. Keep the octopus in your freezer sealed in a plastic bag for two weeks or more so that it is tenderised. Thaw overnight.'

Jean-Michel continued to smile as he lifted the octopus out of the fridge.

'Turn the body of the octopus inside out, like so, and remove the entrails.'

The TV chef demonstrated what needed to be done.

'Now clean it thoroughly, turn the body right side out and remove the beak and the soft surround.'

Again Jean-Michel Starr showed the camera what he was doing.

'Gently simmer the octopus in water having added onion and bay leaves.'

He showed the pan containing the octopus boiling lightly next to an identical pan which also contained an octopus

'Do this for about an hour as I have done with this other octopus then take the pulpo out of the water and cut off the tentacles and slice them like this.'

Jean-Michel Starr showed how he thinly sliced the tentacle on the diagonal.

'Now cut up the body into pieces of a similar size to the cut tentacles, place all of the pulpo onto pre-warmed serving plate, sprinkle with cayenne and paprika. Drizzle heated olive oil over the pulpo, add salt to taste and serve with crusty bread. Voilà : Pulpo en el carnaval.'

The second the director had shouted "cut" and the camera was no longer on him, the smile left Jean-Michel's handsome face.

'Next time, you stinking camera man,' cried Jean-Michel, sticking his finger into the man's chest. 'Do not poke the camera right in my face, do not get in my way when I go to the refrigerator and do not film me from my left. Film my right side! That is my better side. Do you understand?'

Jean-Michel flounced over to the director leaving the cameraman mouthing to the sound crew one word...'Bitch!'

'And for you, peaches,' Jean-Michel Starr put his face right up against the director's. 'I never want to see you again. I shall get a new director appointed immediately.'

The TV director sighed. Working for prima donnas like Starr was never easy. No, it was not easy at all.

*

'Yes,' agreed Peter Mingan. 'Magic does sound as if it could be involved.'

'So you think that one of the magic wielders from Faerie could easily take on the image of another person and charm them, as appears to have happened in the case of Marianne Foxleigh?' Superintendent Penny Graves was checking the notes she had made.

'No problem at all,' stated the werewolf. 'Many folk from Faerie could do that. There are many past masters of illusion and quite a number of shape-changers who can do better than I can.'

'You can change from a man into a wolf?'

'That's right,' laughed the werewolf. 'All lycanthropes can do that.'

'Can you turn into a different man than the one you are?' she queried.

'Only by acting a part, not by illusion,' answered the werewolf.

'But many Faerie folk can?'

'Not werewolves,' he stressed. 'We do get a bad history, I'm afraid, but this one is not down to werewolves.'

'I wasn't suggesting werewolves might have done this or that they are involved in any way,' Penny hastened to reassure him although secretly that was just what she had been thinking. 'But who would you suggest could do this?'

'Fairies, wizards, dragons, some elves,' he replied. 'Even some dwarves. You mustn't, however, assume that a wielder of magic must come from Faerie.'

'Why not?' Penny asked.

'Since the clashing of worlds occurred there are plenty of Earth's own minions who can manage magic like this,' answered Mingan.

'Such as?' asked the policewoman.

'Such as the demigods or the angels.'

'Demigods?'

'Dagon, the money god defeated by Jimmy Scott, was a demigod who could shape-change,' replied the werewolf. 'Nothing to do with faerie apart from the magical power that resulted from the clashing of worlds.'

'Are there other demigods and gods?' Penny asked incredulous.

'Scores of them,' replied the ambassador from the Faerie Reality.

'Scores?'

'From Aah the old Egyptian moon god of time to Zeus who ruled Olympus,' replied Peter Mingan. 'And all the others in between.'

'And they are all now active on Earth?' Penny's eyes bulged with surprise and horror.

'No, no,' Peter waved his rather hairy hands. 'Don't get me wrong. They're just potentially active. They did not all exist or have not all survived.'

'But even a few of them could make life unbearable,' Penny

flapped her hands. 'It's been bad enough with the few that have turned up.'

'I agree,' answered Mingan. 'But it is best that you know the truth.'

'Are there no rules in this magic business?' asked Penny. 'Because if there are not we could be in for a very difficult time.'

'There are rules, of course,' answered Mingan. 'But it is finding out what they are that is difficult. Many of the demi-gods are or were benign, if rather capricious. Fairies are good at illusion but not actual shape changing. Dragons are the most intelligent of the lot. Magic is usually countered by simple iron and Jimmy Scott found out that magnetic monopoles were involved in this.'

'You mentioned the angels,' continued Penny, still looking at her list. 'Could they have arranged the disappearances and utilised shape changing in this way. Could Jimmy Scott have done this?'

'Could he have done this?' repeated the werewolf. 'He has the power so the answer is yes but knowing the man as I do the conclusion is no. This was not the work of the angels.'

'Well that's one lot ruled out,' said Penny with some relief, putting a line through the word angels.

'Unless you include the fallen angels otherwise known as demons,' added Mingan. 'They could and would do any of this.'

'Oh sugar!' Penny wrote another line with demons on it. 'Do you think they did?'

'Not really,' answered the werewolf contemplating the question. 'At present Jimmy Scott is guarding their leader and it is from him that most of their power emanates.'

'You mean Lucifer?'

'Indeed. Lucifer, Beelzebub, Satan. He has the power and the motive but he is not at loose.'

'You are sure of this?'

'I've checked with Scott. Satan is bound in Hell.'

Penny crossed a few more names off her list.

'So where do we go from here?' she asked. 'How can we eliminate anybody when there are so many possibilities?'

'I'd like to go down to Bristol and chat to some of your team who have been looking into the disappearances. Try to determine how the illusionist or shape-changer might have discovered Marianne Foxleigh's secret desire in a lover.'

'Well he did manage to look like her live-in partner,' exclaimed Penny Graves.

'From whom she was estranged emotionally,' answered the werewolf. 'I suspect that the person who did this can also read minds.'

'Read minds?' Penny groaned.

'No, don't be upset,' the werewolf tried to cheer her up. 'That's not a bad thing.'

'Why not?'

'Because the number of Faerie folk and magic-wielding Earth dwellers who can both shape change and read minds is strictly limited.'

'Have you dismissed the illusionists?' Penny queried, again checking her notes.

'Careful examination of the videos at no time shows a slip-up on the part of the perpetrator,' answered Mingan. 'That is very difficult for an illusionist to achieve. They can fool the one they are with but also fooling all the cameras all of the time....that's a major challenge.'

'So who are the wielders of magic who can do this?' asked Penny, brightening a little.

'If it is a shape changer and if they can read minds,' the werewolf was speaking slowly gathering his thoughts. 'And I stress the word if .... then we have just a few possible culprits.'

'Who are they?'

'The golden dragons, some of the more powerful fairies, a couple of dwarves and some of your own demigods.'

'So which of those would you put your bet on?' asked Penny, trying to pin the werewolf down a little.

'Me?' asked the werewolf. 'I'd wager it was either disgruntled fairies or some of your own demigods who are involved. We won't know who until we can determine the motive or motives.'

'So you don't think these are just random attacks on vulnerable people at conferences?'

'Do you?' asked Mingan in a surprised voice. 'If this one example is anything to go on there must have been considerable preparation. The man didn't just randomly attack Foxleigh he arranged to meet her and shaped himself like her heart's desire.'

'Do you think she is still alive?'

'Not in this reality,' replied the werewolf. 'No. I believe that Marianne is dead and I also think that the missing professionals are deceased.'

'What makes you say that?' asked Penny.

'I believe your police say that missing persons either don't want to be discovered or they are usually found fairly quickly, dead or alive.'

'There are exceptions, of course,' replied Penny. 'But as a rule that is the case.'

'None of these people have been found and they are a highly unlikely bunch to be in hiding,' answered the werewolf. 'They were at the top of their professions with good salaries and they would not like to remain missing. They are not runaway children.'

'So you think they are dead?'

'Or in another dimension,' answered the werewolf. 'Though I would not hold out too much hope for the latter.'

*

The Darkness Lounge Bar in Soho was one of Jean-Michel Starr's favourite joints. He stood sipping a very pleasant pink gin and observing the scene in front of him. A gay couple were writhing in a cage, a trim muscular man was cavorting on a trapeze and two ladies were wrestling in mud.

Starr approved. This was just what he needed as therapy after his gruelling TV show.

And he might just score.

I usually do, he thought to himself.

Ten minutes later, his pink gin almost finished, Jean-Michel was beginning to think that he might have to buy himself a second drink, something almost unheard of, when someone tapped him on the shoulder.

A strong, muscular young man, tanned and healthy, was standing next to him sporting a very quizzical look on his rugged face.

'Would you like a top up?' asked the owner of the tapping finger. 'And if so what is your tipple? What would you fancy?'

Giving the young man a look that clearly replied that the man was his fancy, Jean-Michel asked for a pink gin. Within moments they were deep in conversation about cooking. The man gave his name as Dylan and told Jean-Michel that he was a costume designer for the National Ballet.

'But there is no need for you to tell me who you are,' continued Dylan. 'You are the celebrity chef, Jean-Michel Starr. I adore your programme. Simply adore it!'

Jean-Michel lapped up the flattery taking it as merely what was owed to him and he soon accepted an invitation to Dylan's home.

'We have to go by car but it is not all that far,' explained Dylan as he led Jean-Michel to a beautiful Bentley Continental.

'You'll have to take me back home to Hampstead after I have seen your house,' murmured Jean-Michel.

'Of course,' replied Dylan. 'It will be my pleasure.'

The house was in Petherton Road, Islington, where Jean-Michel knew, from experience, a small one-bedroom flat could cost more than half a million pounds. This young man apparently owned the whole house. Jean-Michel found it very curious.

The young costume designer has to be seriously rich so he has clearly not picked me up for my money, thought Jean-Michel. Because of his celebrity status this was a constant hazard for Starr and he always worried about it. *Maybe he really does want to get to know me better?*

While Dylan prepared some drinks Jean-Michel preened himself in the mirror. There was just a little silver in his dark hair but he looked at this and thought that all it did was make him look more distinguished. His face had that slightly haughty aristocratic appearance with the high cheekbones and slim aquiline nose that some lucky Frenchmen possessed. Jean-Michel knew that people admired his looks and so found no difficulty in admiring them himself.

Of course his name was not really Jean-Michel Starr. He had chosen that name because of the inherent suggestion that his restaurant deserved a Michelin star.... and it had worked.

His previous incarnation as a sous-chef at the Beefeater in Crewe had been getting him nowhere and he had made the life-changing decision to jettison his old circle of friends, claim to be a celebrity chef from Paris and get on television. He now had ten restaurants and a range of products named after him...something that would surely not have happened if he had stuck with his original name of Bert Adcock.

'Here are the drinks,' Dylan took Jean-Michel's mind away from his own past history and back to the present. 'Try taking it down in one. It's quite special.'

The celebrity chef threw the strange coloured cocktail down his throat in one gulp. The taste was strange, slightly salty like tequila but inherently pleasant.

'Would you like another?' asked his host, genially waving a jug around.

'Certainly,' agreed Jean-Michel.

He could already feel the drink hitting him and it occurred that Dylan would not be able to give him a lift home if he had also drunk the cocktail. He watched as another two glasses were downed. Dylan certainly would not be able to drive....not only because he would be beyond the legal limit but also because it would not be safe to trust an important person, a celebrity chef no less, to the hands of a chauffeur who was even the slightest bit incapacitated by the influence of alcohol.

Before he could frame a sensible question Dylan replied as if reading his mind.

'Don't worry,' said Dylan. 'I won't need to drive. You'll be staying for supper.'

'I didn't realise you were having me for supper as well as for a drink,' remarked the chef.

'Oh yes,' replied Dylan. 'And I'm sure you will enjoy helping me to prepare it.'

'Will I?' asked Jean-Michel.

Now he certainly was surprised. To be honest he did not really like doing any of the real work. In the restaurants he had sous-chefs organising and running everything. He just put his name to the menus which consisted of dishes which he had "borrowed" from other cooks' recipe books. The TV programme was no different. He did not prepare any of the food that was shown on the programme...the work was all done by poorly paid researchers or interns who worked long hours and received no pay at all.

'Yes you will,' replied Dylan firmly.

'Yes I will,' Jean-Michel heard himself say.

'Now we are going to prepare your speciality dish,' explained Dylan. 'Your signature recipe. Which is, if you remember, Pulpo en el carnaval?'

'Yes,' smiled Jean-Michel, thinking that at least he could remember that dish. He had been recording a new programme about it that very afternoon so he should remember.

'So what do we need?' asked Dylan.

'Onion, bay, paprika, cayenne pepper, olive oil, sea salt flakes,' replied Jean-Michel.

'Yes,' agreed Dylan. 'That's right. It's a recipe you stole from Rick Stein. He called it Pulpo à la feria. is that right?'

'Yes,' agreed Jean-Michel, smiling warmly at Dylan. 'That's exactly what I did!'

What's happening to me? wondered Starr. *I never admit things like that to anyone. It's professional suicide!*

'And your real name isn't even Jean-Michel Starr, is it?' asked Dylan.

'No,' replied Starr. 'I'm really Bertram Adcock from Barnsley.'

'But there is one ingredient you have left out of the recipe, isn't there, Bertram?' asked Dylan.

'The octopus?' smiled Jean-Michel.

'Yes the octopus,' agreed Dylan. 'And we have all the rest of the ingredients but we don't have a suitable dead octopus. So what shall we do?'

'Find something else such as a a squid?' asked Jean-Michel.

'We don't have a squid and we don't have a cuttlefish. Or even other highly intelligent species such as a chimpanzee or gorilla,' said Dylan. 'Or whale meat for that matter. So I have a good idea. Why don't we replace the octopus with Jean-Michel Starr.'

'Me?' asked the chef, beginning now to be very worried but unable to voice a significant protest and, now when he tried, unable to move anything apart from his lungs.

'Yes you. Do you have any problems with that?'

'It wouldn't be Pulpo en el carnaval,' he managed to gasp.

'Nor will it be Pulpo à la feria,' replied Dylan. 'I think we could call it Homo sapiens à la feria perhaps, or maybe we should drop the sapiens. You're not a very wise species are you? Not very wise at all.'

Jean-Michel looked at Dylan uncomprehendingly. What was

really going on? Why could he no longer feel his feet or hands? Why was he finding it difficult to breathe?

*

It was late in the afternoon before Cranbrook awoke, despite the anaesthetic supposedly being a short acting one. Williams had not liked to interfere with the patient in any way and it was possible that Cranbrook had simply been sleeping for a good part of the time. The anaesthetist had stuck around, whistling happily to himself but all of the other staff had disappeared, the senior surgeon muttering as he went that he would chivvy up the CEO's response.

Tim Cranbrook looked at the policeman with surprise.

'Am I pleased to see you?' he remarked.

'I don't know,' answered Williams. 'Are you? Most people around here don't seem to be.'

'And I've still got a brain,' smiled Cranbrook. 'Is there any way you can get me out of this place? I did not give consent to come here and I want to get out.'

Williams looked at the anaesthetist who simply shrugged his shoulders.

'It's OK with me,' replied the gas man. 'I only work here. I don't make the rules.'

'Are there any strong wheelchairs in this place?' asked Cranbrook. 'Something that I can propel with one arm?'

'I doubt it,' answered the anaesthetist. 'There are wheelchairs but they are the sort that the porters push around.'

'I'll allow the big copper to push me,' said Cranbrook.

'You'll have to hurry,' remarked the anaesthetist. 'The CEO will return with the security team any minute. The surgeon has gone to get her.'

'Which security team?' asked DS Johnson. 'They didn't do much good so far.'

'The security is contracted out to a private firm,' replied the gas man. 'What they lack in efficiency they make up for in sheer bloody mindedness, contempt for authority outside of their own and fire power.'

'Then we had better get a move on,' suggested Cranbrook. 'Are you coming with us?'

The latter question was directed at the anaesthetist.

'Me? No way,' replied the doctor. 'I'm an out and out Vicar of Bray.'

'Meaning that you side with whoever is in the position of power?' asked Daniel Williams.

'That's right... and when the security team get here I'll tell them exactly where you have gone.'

'I'm sure you will not do that,' replied Williams. The big policeman turned to DS Johnson and winked, the gesture obviously visible to the gas man. 'I'll phone for the police helicopter and we'll meet them on the roof.'

'Right boss!' agreed Johnson with alacrity.

'I'm assuming that there is a helipad on the roof?' Williams directed this question to the doctor.

'There is,' the anaesthetist replied. 'And it is on the top of this particular building. Not the other blocks.'

'Then that's where we are heading. Don't tell anyone!' Williams winked again, this time at the doctor then helped the huge invalid onto the strongest looking of the wheelchairs and pushed him out of the suite, down the corridor and into a lift, followed by DS Johnson.

The gas man walked off into the changing room, a rather small and bedraggled figure.

'Where are we really going?' asked Johnson.

'To the roof,' replied Williams.

'But the anaesthetist knows that you have no hope of getting the police helicopter here in time,' replied Johnson.

'So he'll believe that we are going to the ground floor or

basement,' countered Williams. 'And we will send the lift back down to the basement as soon as we get out of it.'

'But he'd be right about the police helicopter,' continued Johnson. 'They really are impossible to contact unless they're forewarned.'

'True,' replied the large detective. 'But I did take the liberty of asking the air ambulance man if he might help and he agreed that he would if there were no new disasters.....and while we wait the big boy here can tell me what he was going to say when the care team burst in and stopped him in the nursing home in Bristol. What do you say to that, Tim?'

'I'll do that boss!' agreed Cranbrook. 'But I'm not so sure that my name is Tim.'

'I'm coming with you too,' said the small quavering voice of the cleaning lady. She had not left with the other staff but had remained with them the whole time, keeping very still and quiet.

'It wouldn't be healthy for me to stay here much longer,' the figure said with a grin and as she spoke she changed into a slight, beautiful girl with pointed ears.

'My sprite!' exclaimed Cranbrook. 'I thought that you had been crushed to death!'

'That's what I hoped Whittington would think,' remarked the sprite. 'I created the illusion of myself walking into the cave.'

'But what about the horrible monster you became?' asked Cranbrook.

'That was Whittington's own illusion overlaying mine,' answered Lah Lah.

The elevator had reached the roof and now they were waiting for a helicopter.

'So what were you going to tell us?' asked Williams.

'All I can recall is that I watched a TV programme about lost or missing professional folk and they wanted any clues people could give them and I was fascinated that the attacks had all occurred close to a large river or by the sea....and I thought that magic might be involved. That's it, then it's all a blur,' replied Cranbrook.

The whup, whup , whup of the approaching chopper could be heard very loudly but also the sound of the lift returning.

They loaded Cranbrook onto the helicopter and the machine took off just as soon as the last person had jumped in. As the chopper rose into the air shots rang out from the vicinity of the elevator.

'They certainly do play rough,' Williams felt obliged to agree with the anaesthetist. 'And they do suffer from sheer bloody mindedness.'

But they were well away and nobody was hurt.

Chapter 12

Dr. Martin Threadneedle walked arrogantly along the corridor of the London teaching hospital. He was only a second year foundation house officer but he was certainly a confident one. He enjoyed the life of a doctor: the respect from the patients, the admiring glances from the nursing staff, the way in which his utterances at parties were given credence that the opinions of others did not get. In addition he was near the end of his two foundation years and he would soon, in just three more weeks of work and three weeks of terminal vacation, be registered and licensed.

Then he would be away from the hospital and into a very well paid research job in the multi-billion dollar pharmaceutical company that his family owned.

The one thing he would not miss was the way in which people made jokes about his name. They always assumed that Dr. Threadneedle was going to be a surgeon and that, consequently, he could not wait to deal with any wound that appeared in the overworked accident and emergency department. That was not the direction his career would take. In his intercalated bachelor of science degree he had studied the pharmacological activity of the dark ink ejected by squids when alarmed. The substance was toxic to some tumour cells and had other interesting properties. In addition he had watched squids as they fought predators. The ink acted as both an alarm system and a smokescreen. In addition the creatures being attacked would eject smaller clouds of ink with greater mucous content. These were known as pseudomorphs or false bodies and kept their shape longer than the usual clouds of ink. The size of the pseudomorph mimicked the size of the ink-squirting cephalopod itself and predators, such as eels and turtles, had been seen to attack the pseudomorphs rather than the squid. Meanwhile the squid would change colour and jet off to safety.

So his first research idea when he was employed by the family firm would be to continue his work on the very interesting inks.

It was the fact that the nurse of the respiratory ward had not made a joke about his name that had endeared her to Dr. Threadneedle. He had invited her to his room when his ward round had finished, telling her about the mess beer-drinking society.

'We all chip in a few pounds each week,' he had explained. 'And keep a supply of real ale in our mess room. Even the management chip in. So would you like to sample a tipple?'

She had fixed him with a totally enchanting stare and then replied very simply.

'Yes!'

'OK,' he had then asked her. 'I'll be finished at five-thirty. Would that be OK?'

She had agreed that it would.

At five-thirty on the dot he met her on the ward and, smiling and laughing, they walked up the stairs of the old building and into the doctor's mess. None of the other doctors had finished their day yet which Martin Threadneedle knew was due to their general inefficiency compared with himself.

He led the young nurse to his room and she sat on the bed whilst he ran back to the mess bar to pick up a couple of pints of the latest real ale that they had on tap.

Careful not to spill any of the foaming drinks but very eager to return to the girl he hurried back to his room. To his surprise she had already kicked off her shoes and was lying out on the bed.

'You actually do have some beers in your mess,' she said in a surprised voice. 'I thought that was only a chat up line.'

Putting the beers on his dressing table Martin turned his

attention to the girl.

He kissed her on the lips. The girl not only looked good, she also tasted fantastic!

'Now for those beers,' she said after they had kissed and cuddled. 'And we'll see how you get on after that.'

They downed the beers.

'Not bad for a beginning,' she whispered. 'Now we shall go for a meal and we will see what you can do with added strength.'

The couple slipped out of the hospital to a nearby take-away as she had declared that she would be very happy with a kebab.

Back in his room she quickly ate the food and then wanted to get into a clinch with Martin again.

Martin was amazed. He had finally found what he had always been looking for...a willing, beautiful nymphomaniac who liked beer and kebabs...and she was all his!

She started to kiss him on his fingertips and the sensation was compelling. Then he felt something warm around his legs. He looked down anxiously.

'It's only a sleeping bag,' whispered the girl. 'I thought you might like to get really cosy inside one.'

Where did she get that from? wondered Martin. *Was it in the cupboard.*

Of course not, silly, came the telepathic reply. *It's not really a sleeping bag. It's part of little old me engulfing your body.*

Martin laughed at the joke as the sleeping bag seemed to independently wrap itself around his body and nestle into his neck. Just his head and the nurse's were poking out of the soft engulfing cocoon.

Gradually she ingested both his legs, his crutch, his torso and Martin just lay back with a look of ecstasy on his face. He did not even notice when the monstrous creature shed its female image completely and swallowed him whole. In his dreams as he died he was completely happy and completely satisfied.

*

The small hotel near the zoo was in a grade 2 listed building. The room was clean but small and perfectly adequate. The place did serve evening meals but Kurt, after lying down for a few minutes to rest his feet, decided to go out for a walk on the Downs, the huge park area in the middle of the city.

The walk took him back past the zoo and to the Sea Walls. He had forgotten how magnificent the panorama was from the viewing point. Kurt was able to see all the way out to the Bristol Channel and across to Wales and, in the opposite direction, to the magnificent structure of Isambard Kingdom Brunel's suspension bridge.

He stood up close to the railings and looked down at the Avon hundreds of feet below him. It was half full due to the controversial Severn tidal barrage. Kurt considered the arguments which were still raging about the effect the barrage had on the environment and the loss of the unique wildlife habitats. He ruefully remembered the fact that he would never witness the Severn Bore. To see the Bore with his own eyes had been one of his minor ambitions as he was aware that it had been one of Britain's spectacular natural phenomena: a large surge wave that people could actually surf. Not the biggest in the world, he thought that accolade went to a river in China, but it had been spectacular all the same and he had only seen it on television.

'Fabulous view isn't it?' said a man standing to his right.

'Yes it is,' agreed Kurt and, as the man moved closer to him, he added. 'Do I know you?'

'I was at the meeting,' stated the fellow. 'Your lecture was excellent. Would you like to go for a drink? Or into the woods?'

Kurt stared at the man in outright amazement and moved away.

The second time today, he thought, *but this time it's a man. The lecture was good but not that good. What in Heaven's name is going* on? These people in Bristol are as bad as the sirens in my story to the kids.

Milly and Molly came into his mind, laughing uproariously at his jokes and his awful singing.

'I don't think I would like to go with you into any woods,' Kurt replied, moving even further away.

'I think you should,' said the man, trying to entice Kurt.

'Think what you like mate,' replied Kurt as he broke into a run, trying to get away from the beguiling person. 'But I'm not going anywhere with you.'

The man started to follow Kurt but the presence of other people out strolling and running put him off and Kurt soon lost him. Even still Kurt could not stop getting the impression that he was being watched and found himself glancing over his shoulder to check that he was not being followed.

He took a lonely meal in a pleasant enough Italian restaurant on Whiteladies Road, sitting with his back to a wall, warily watching that nobody came to close to him, before he headed back to his hotel for an early night. After locking the door he wedged a chair under the door handle and then closed all the windows and bolted them. He had no idea how the guy had found him and it had occurred to Kurt that someone could have followed him from the zoo to the hotel. If so they would not have to run after him as they would know where to find him.

Before going to sleep he telephoned Sally. They had a muted conversation in which he told her the meeting had gone very well but that he was missing her and the girls. He did not mention his fears regarding the man on the Downs and in retrospect also the young lady at the zoo but did promise to call earlier the next evening so that he could speak to the girls before they went to bed.

*

'So you really can't tell us any more?' asked DCI Williams.

They had landed in Bristol on the top of the Southmead Hospital. Williams wanted the medics that he knew to have a look at the man before he was released to a nursing home of his choice. Cranbrook had been given a room to himself in the relatively new hospital which had luckily sustained no damage during the recent cataclysmic clash of realities.

Williams and Johnson were going over all that had happened with Cranbrook and they had reached, once again, the point where he had told them that he believed water and magic were implicated in the disappearances. However the fact that most people lived near water was not news to Williams. Had all of this been a wild goose chase?

'I'm sure that there was more but I just don't remember,' replied Cranbrook, shaking his head. 'I have a constant feeling that I should be able to help you and that this sort of thing has happened before but I can't explain it. My mind is clouded.'

'Why did you say that you are not sure that your name is Tim?' asked DS Johnson, consulting his notebook.

Sid Johnson had long ago discovered that writing things into a notebook not only focussed his own mind and acted as an aide memoire but it also focussed the attention of the person being questioned.

'Because his name isn't Tim,' the sprite replied for him.

Lah Lah had a surprising ability to go unnoticed if she wished. Despite her outstandingly beautiful appearance she could merge into the background and then startle the occupants of the room when they realised that she was still there.

Why was she still there? This had gone through Williams mind as a question several times. Perhaps now he would find out?

'So what is his name?' asked the big policeman. 'And why can he not remember it?'

'He doesn't normally tell people his name even when he is completely well,' answered Lah Lah. 'And he doesn't remember because he has been affected by several amnesic hexes which I had hoped would wear off by now.'

She looked at the big invalid who was absorbed in the act of trying to wiggle his toes. His concentration was so great that he did not observe them all looking at him. His toes had moved! They really had.

'My toes have moved!' exclaimed Cranbrook delightedly.

'Yes,' said Williams rather drily. 'But we were asking why you thought that Tim was not your name.'

'Because it isn't!' exclaimed Cranbrook. 'It's not even Cranbrook. I know that for sure now. But you don't understand the significance of this. I haven't been able to move them at all for months!'

'Probably years,' Lah Lah corrected him.

'Do you really think it's years?' he asked, raising his right hand in a questioning manner and then looking at it in astonishment. This was the arm that had been paralysed.

'I'm convinced of it,' replied the sprite. 'And at last my healing magic is beginning to work.'

'This is all beyond me,' sighed Sid Johnson, running his hand through his hair. 'So who are you?'

'That I don't know,' replied Cranbrook ruefully. 'I know the answer is in my head somewhere but I just can't remember. I wish I could.....'

'I believe that I do,' Lah Lah interrupted the big invalid who was once again marvelling at the way that he was regaining movement in his feet.

'Tell us!' demanded Williams.

'I want him to remember for himself,' replied the sprite. 'Otherwise the cure may be incomplete.'

'Then whisper it in my ear,' ordered the detective chief inspector.

'OK,' replied Lah Lah and she bounced over to where

the policeman was standing on the other side of the bed and whispered quietly in his right ear.

'Really?' Williams was nonplussed. 'I thought that he was a myth or perhaps an ancient hero who had died.'

'No,' answered the sprite. 'I know him well because he was married to my sister.'

'Who is he?' asked Johnson impatiently.

'I can't tell you out loud, as the young lady said it might damage him,' Williams stated. 'And you'll find it hard to believe the answer but if you come over here I will whisper in your ear like this lady did in mine.'

'I know who I would prefer whispering in my ear,' grumbled Johnson. 'And it's not you!'

Williams looked just a little miffed that his junior officer felt happy to insult him in this way but before he could say anything Cranbrook spoke.

'You can all stop whispering and talking about me in the third person,' said the large man, now freely moving his legs. 'I heard what the wood elf whispered in your ear, DCI Williams, and the knowledge has not harmed my mind and I do now remember. She is right. I am who she says I am.'

He jumped off the bed and stood flexing his enormous muscles. Now, standing tall, he clearly towered over Daniel Williams who was, in himself, a very large man.

'Yes,' continued the person they had known as Tim Cranbrook. 'I am indeed the one she has been looking for. I am the ancient hero, the demigod some know as Hercules and others called Heracles.'

Then he sat down again on the bed.

'But you can call me Harry, if you like,' his voice had lost the booming quality it had adopted and he was speaking like a normal person. 'And I appear to have lost about five years of my life. What on Earth has been happening?'

*

Kurt was standing in front of the lions' cage at the zoo. On one side of him stood the man who had spoken to him on the Downs and on the other the young lady from the conference. As he looked at them they morphed into ugly animal shapes. One became a hippopotamus and the other a lion, larger than the ones in the cage. Kurt was unable to run, his feet were stuck to the tarmac. The lion, a strange mauve colour that made Kurt feel queasy just to look at, moved in on him from one side and the hippo from the other. It was a race to see which would swallow him first. Kurt recalled that hippos killed more people than any other large animal so he tried to move towards the lion. It was to no avail and they both chomped down on him. The lion took his left arm and the hippo his right, each pulling as hard as they could. His arms stretched out, further and further, impossibly so as the two fierce animals pulled on him. Then a score of monkeys appeared and started dancing a tango which turned into a good impression of the can-can, he found himself singing along to the tune and the twins started laughing at his bad vocal efforts.

It was at this point that Kurt realised he was dreaming. He sat up in the bed with an awful jolt, his heart was pounding and he was sweating profusely. He turned on the light and looked round the room. There was nothing out of place but he could tell that outside the night breeze had turned into a sudden summer squall and he could hear the howling of the wind followed by heavy rainfall. In the distance he thought he could detect the roar of a lion at the zoo and he decided that this had prompted his nightmare.

He settled back down to sleep not at all sure that he wanted to go to the conference in the morning. Unfortunately although he was not speaking again he was on a panel for a quiz session so knew that he could not go awol. Eventually he slept deeply without dreaming.

*

Tuesday morning dawned and Hercules had been checked out by the Southmead physicians. They pronounced him to be amazingly fit, finding it astonishing that he had been paralysed for so long but was now so well. The huge demigod agreed to meet the police team at the central police station where they had the incident room but first he wanted to speak to little Lah Lah. She was nowhere to be seen but returned just before the hero was leaving to travel to the police station. Williams had decided that he would pick the huge man up on the principle that he and Johnson had done so much to find the guy it would be stupid to lose him at this point in the proceedings.

'Before I go,' boomed Hercules to Lah Lah. 'I need to know about your sister. How is she? How is my most favourite and most beautiful wife for whom I have a longing, a love, a desire more than anything in either of the realities?'

The great hero smiled at Lah Lah expecting a favourable report.

'She is dead,' replied the wood elf in a flat voice. 'She was killed by Parsifal X and you were not there to defend her.'

'Dead!' cried Hercules, totally distraught. 'Dead? But I only left her a few weeks ago and I promised to return. Now she is dead! This cannot be so!'

'Somebody got the better of you and nearly killed you,' remarked Williams. 'And that would have been just at the time that Parsifal X was invading Earth.'

'So he is likely to be behind this ghastly charade, this incarceration, this unholy imprisonment!' the voice of the truly huge man became louder with each imprecation. 'I shall find him and kill him. He has made an enemy of the immortal hero Hercules and he shall be made to pay!'

'Too late to do that,' remarked Williams. 'He was sorted out by Jimmy Scott and his mother-in-law.'

'Who are they?' asked Hercules, confused yet again.

'That's another story,' replied the detective. 'We better get a move on if we are to meet the other policemen.'

'Have you no feelings, man?' asked Hercules. 'I have just lost my wife!'

'That is true and I am sorry,' replied Williams. 'But there are people right now who are in danger of losing their loved ones and we may be the only people who can help.'

'You don't understand how I feel,' cried the huge hero. 'You can't appreciate my anguish.'

'Unfortunately I can,' replied Williams. 'You see, I lost my wife and my only daughter when the two worlds collided. It was a massive disaster and no-one was left untouched.'

'Someone has to pay. Someone has to be held to account,' cried Hercules, calming down but his eyes bulging with anger and grief combined.

'You are right and the persons who incarcerated you and kept you controlled as a paralysed invalid are still at large,' stated Williams. 'And we must find them and stop them from harming more people.'

'You are right,' agreed the hero, deflated by the loss of emotion. 'I was being selfish and hotheaded. Alack it is often my way but we must work on.'

'Now can you see why I said what I did to you?' asked the wood sprite.

'Which thing you said to me?' asked Hercules. 'You've said quite a lot.'

'I said I would l love you or leave you, cure you or kill you,' she replied. 'I thought you had purposely deserted my sister and deserved to die.'

'The grief is so hard to bear I wish you had killed me,' replied the hero. 'Though, since I am immortal, that does not appear to be an easy thing to do.'

'Which is why their spells only kept you partially paralysed, I imagine,' surmised Williams. 'And also why your musculature did not atrophy as it would have done with a mere mortal. But now it is getting close to clobberin' time.'

'That's the Hulk, not Hercules,' replied Lah Lah, with a slight pout.

'I don't even think it's the Hulk,' answered Hercules. 'I reckon the quote is from Ben Grimm, aka the Thing.'

'Who?' asked Williams.

'The big, ugly orange-coloured rocky one in the Fantastic Four,' replied the ancient superhero. 'He's a fictional character from a comic.'

'Oh,' replied Williams. 'I thought the line was original.'

Chapter 13

The morning session at the conference in the Bristol Zoological Gardens had gone very well. Kurt had sat on the quiz panel and acquitted himself adequately. He would not have marked himself as excellent but nobody likes a smart-arse so the occasional slip on a conference quiz panel did no harm.

At the coffee break nobody came up and tried to proposition him and by lunchtime Kurt had almost forgotten his funk of the previous day. Nightmares about shape-changing monsters seemed ridiculous in the light of day.

He did, however, decide to go for a walk to Clifton Village over lunch rather than round the zoo. He was enjoying window shopping on The Mall, looking at the jewellers, the musical instruments, wine stores and then round the corner studying various antiques. The Big Issue salesman offered him a copy and he gave the man the correct money.

'Can you spare any change?' asked a beggar who had squatted down next to the Big Issue man. 'Change for a poor homeless man.'

'Don't give him any,' the Big Issue man was annoyed. 'I've never seen the blighter before and he is queering my pitch.'

'Can't he also work selling the Big Issue?' asked Kurt.

'He could if he was really homeless,' replied the magazine salesman. 'But he only arrived here just before you did and somebody dropped him off from a new Jaguar.'

The rumbled beggar moved away scowling, changing his appearance when he was round the corner.

The walk had been rather spoilt so Kurt hurried back to the meeting, ready for the fray of the afternoon session. Once again

Kurt did not notice that he was being followed.

*

'So what do we have?' asked Penny Graves.

The big noticeboard in the incident room was covered with photographs of the missing professionals. It was clear that a large number were scientists but not all of them.

The superintendent policewoman continued.

'The count of missing professionals is now up to sixty-seven and more are missing each day,' she paused for breath. 'Unofficially it is nearer to six hundred and none of the other teams around the world are near to solving the mystery. None of the missing have been found and no messages have been received so we can rule out kidnapping for money and extortion.'

There was a gasp at the mention of the larger figure. Penny Graves looked round the room at the assembled policemen plus Hercules, Lah Lah the sprite, Peter Mingan the werewolf and Rick Passmore, the missing scientist's house partner.

'But we have two possible leads both suggesting that magic has been involved,' she added. 'The first was the call from Tim Cranbrook who has now turned out to be Hercules. According to his wife's sister, Lah Lah, who is with us today, he has been missing for five years. It is that timeframe which has allowed us to increase the missing number so dramatically.'

'How does Hercules fit into the pattern of missing professionals?' asked DCI Jim Rogers, intrigued by the narrative.

'He was apparently at a meeting for retired naval captains when he went missing,' replied Graves. 'That is retired from active service in the US Navy, in which role he had received the Medal of Honor.'

Hercules looked just a little abashed.

'It's usually easier to be brave if you are immortal and extremely strong,' he muttered embarrassedly.

'Maybe,' agreed Graves. 'But you are brave, nevertheless.'

Hercules now went quite scarlet to the roots of his wiry red hair.

'I shall continue,' said Penny Graves. 'The other lead is that Dame Marianne Foxleigh was courted by a man who looked uncannily like her former lover. This we know because of the multiple cameras that recorded footage of the two of them in London.'

Graves paused for this to sink in.

'And when I say the man looked uncannily like her former lover I really do mean that. Yet her former lover, Dr. Rick Passmore, was incontrovertibly one hundred and twenty miles away from the scene. We have eye-witness statements to that effect and even some digital photographs, sent to us by another participant at the dinner Rick attended in Bristol. He is here with us, stand up please Rick.'

The elegant, tall and handsome scientist stood up and took a slightly sarcastic bow. Penny returned to her resumé.

'The disappearance of Dame Marianne Foxleigh was almost undoubtedly due to magic and to support that we have video footage and something that nobody else in this room has known until now.'

This time the pause was simply for dramatic effect.

'We have found her mobile phone in a drain in Soho.'

There was a general murmur of amazement around the room.

'Does the phone reveal anything of importance?' asked Williams.

'Indeed it does and that is what I am about to show the assembled company. There are images in Marianne Foxleigh's photography section on the phone including a video that we have found very hard to interpret but which we think the assembled company might decipher. Lights please!'

Jim Rogers dimmed the lights slightly and the images from the phone appeared on a large flat plasma screen. First there were several selfies of just Marianne Foxleigh as she prepared to go out, then a few more with her date and finally a short, blurred video. The face of the person she was dating appeared to change into a bizarre leech-like monster with a huge mouth. Then the picture tumbled over and over as if the phone had been hurled away as far as the thrower could throw it. Then the picture was very dark until it blacked out completely.

'We believe that the monster attacked Marianne Foxleigh. Unable to fight it, she had the presence of mind to film what was happening and then throw the phone into the drain where the creature could not find it. Lights back up please Jim.'

Rick Passmore was sat with his head in his hands sobbing gently. The huge superhero put his arm round the man and it was clear that Hercules was grieving with him.

'I'm sorry to do this to you, Rick,' said Penny. 'But we have to catch this monster and we needed people to see how much like you the creature was and to see your reaction, in case you had replaced the real Rick Passmore.'

Passmore caught his breath and pulled himself together.

'I entirely understand,' he replied. 'I must have been the most likely suspect. The only thing I would alter in your description is that I believe she would have had the phone in her hand to take a selfie for her first big kiss with the man and that is what she intended filming. The rest is probably as you suggested.'

He sat down very sadly. Williams thought that Passmore was probably reflecting on the fact that the beautiful lady, Marianne Foxleigh, had agreed to a date with a man who looked almost exactly like himself, albeit younger. She had presumably still loved him!

'Does anybody have anything to add to this resumé?' asked Penny.

'Are we sure that the video is not a fake?' asked Jim Rogers. 'Morphing like that into another shape can be done very cleverly these days with computers.'

'The police who found this camera had it looked at professionally and it has not been tampered with,' replied the lady detective.

'It's a miracle that it survived in a drain,' growled Dan Williams. 'My android cellphone was in my pocket. It got wet due to a downpour of rain, made a high-pitched squealing noise like a stuck pig and then refused to work ever again.'

'It is a very special cellphone adapted for underwater use. Divers use them sometimes,' replied Penny. 'Any other comments?'

There was no immediate reply.

'OK, the civilians can leave if they wish,' suggested Graves.

'I'm completely bushed,' said Passmore quietly to Penny Graves, his usual charming manner had returned. 'Would you mind if I called it a day. You know where I can be found. But before I go can I reiterate that I believe the problem is likely to have arisen from the Faerie realm and so I suggest that Peter Mingan asks the various crossing points into Faerie whether they have recently had an unusual traffic of people from Faerie to Earth and vice versa.'

Penny looked towards the werewolf and he nodded agreement.

'Thank you for your help,' Penny replied quite absentmindedly as Passmore got up to go. 'We will let you know about any developments.'

'I'm afraid that I have no accommodation at present so I cannot tell you right now where I shall be staying,' stated Hercules as he rose. 'I'm not in need of a hospital bed any more so I shall have to look for a hotel.'

'No, I imagine you don't need the hospital,' agreed Graves. 'What about you, Lah Lah? Do you have accommodation?'

'I can cope,' replied the sprite.

'I could take both of them to my place. There is plenty of space,' suggested Williams.

'Do that now and come back soon, please,' advised Graves. 'But the rest of the police must stay and we will continue collating information and working through ideas until I call it a day. The civilians can join us tomorrow at nine, here. Any questions?'

Again there were was no immediate clamour so Penny Graves recommended that they had a break and the working party would resume in twenty minutes.

The first thing she intended doing was sending round a notice for all police units to be vigilant and on the look-out for shape-changing creatures attacking human beings. She knew that this would harm her credibility. Until she actually captured one or had better video footage the existence of the monsters would not be believed and the recipients would think she was going soft in the head. Conversely she also knew that she had to send out the warning notice or live with a bad conscience when more people went missing.

*

Just one night and a morning and then I can go back to my family, thought Kurt Collins.

He was walking back to his hotel, much of his fear had receded but he could not prevent himself from looking over his shoulder just occasionally. As he went he tried telephoning his wife. Sally was not answering and he left a short message on her cellphone.

The hotel loomed up ahead and Kurt once more had the tingling feeling between his shoulder blades that made him glance behind. A young female runner in lycra gave him a dirty look, convinced that he was eyeing her form.

Kurt shook his head. What a suspicious world it had become!

Kurt took his key from the reception desk and went up to his room. Everything was in order in the bedroom, the hard-backed upright chair was back in place next to the little table on which the flat screen TV was perched, the bed had been smoothed out by the maid. Kurt looked at the door to the room and admired its strong wood.

One thing about the late Georgian and early Victorian buildings is the quality of the wood, he observed.

He looked at the bathroom door. He knew that the bathroom had to be new…Georgians did not have en-suite facilities unless they were royalty!

If I am being critical, thought Kurt, *the door to the bathroom is a little too thick and the panelling too coarse for a Georgian property. The profile of the wood between the panels should be narrower.*

That did not stop him from using the facilities. When he was comfortable he sat on the bed and sipped a cup of tea. Trying Sally again there was no reply.

A knock came at the door. He opened it gingerly.

'Surprise,' a chorus of three happy voices greeted him.

Standing in the corridor of the hotel were Sally with his twins, Milly and Molly.

'We got the afternoon off school,' Molly said in a bubbly voice.

'And tomorrow is an in-service training day,' added Milly, equally as happy.

'So we've booked the next door room for the twins,' Sally remarked.

'Come in to my humble abode,' Kurt threw the door open wide, pushing down a niggling worry that he could not recall telling Sally exactly which hotel he was staying in. Perhaps he had told her without remembering having done so?

After listening to the girls burbling on about how much fun the maths lesson had been at school Kurt asked them the usual question.

'The long story or the short?'

The girls looked a bit surprised.

'Come on,' smiled Kurt asked. 'Do you want me to tell you the long story about what I have been doing or the short one.'

'Short,' said Molly.

Milly replied the opposite.

'Long...'

'True or false?' asked Kurt

'True!' their reply was a giggle.

'OK,' agreed Collins. 'Moderately long but true.'

Slightly worrying, he pondered, *they usually agree on everything and they always want a false story first.*

Kurt sat on the edge of the bed and the girls sat close to his feet as he told them about the conference, then about the girl and the man who had spoken to him and spooked him and about his bad dream.

The trio sat in rapt attention. In fact they moved closer in as they listened.

'Would you like a song?' he finally asked.

They all looked confused.

'A song?' he queried. 'I always finish with a song.'

'Yes, of course we would like a song,' said Sally. 'Wouldn't we girls?'

'Yes mother,' the girls agreed vociferously.

They normally want a song without prompting. Kurt was worried. This was very strange. He looked at his beautiful wife and his two children and they stared back at him with loving eyes.

'Before I sing the song,' he suggested to the twins. 'Let's do some mental arithmetic. It's your favourite.'

'Yes please,' they chorussed.

'Seven eights?' he cried.

'Fifty six,' they replied instantly.

'Thirteen squared?'

'One hundred and sixty nine,' the reply was even quicker.

That does it, thought Kurt. *This cannot be right. It must be some sort of dream. The girls are only seven years old and they hate mathematics. They could not possibly have got the sums right.*

As he thought this the girls moved closer as if reading his mind. If anything their loving looks became more intense.

Kurt jumped up.

'I usually sing the song with you lying on the floor,' he lied fluently. 'And I stand on the bed.'

He was aware of the fact that he did nothing of the sort but kept the thought away from the top of his mind.

The girls immediately concurred.

Sally usually lies down too, he thought, purposely erroneously. *She's usually the first to lie down.*

To his surprise the twins stood up, Sally lay down and the girls followed her action.

'Now I'm ready,' he stated and started a rendition of Black Cat.

'It's a sunny day
But I cannot feel the sunshine
I consult my stars
I was born under the wrong sign
I'm feeling superstitious
Since I saw a black cat pass my way

My car will not start
So I cannot go out driving
And deep inside my heart
I know bad news is arriving
I'm feeling superstitious
Since I saw a black cat pass my way

I've lost my lucky charm
It should be hanging on my arm

You know just what I mean
Because it's you I haven't seen

Since you went away
My life is filled with sadness
And if you stay away
I'll descend down into madness
I'm feeling superstitious
Since I saw a black cat pass my way
I'm feeling superstitious
Since I saw a black cat pass my way.'

When he stopped the girls and his wife applauded loudly.
'Wonderful,' cried Sally. 'Beautiful singing.'

'More songs please!' cried the twins, speaking together. 'That was beautiful!'

That's something else they never do, he thought very briefly. *They never applaud my singing. They always laugh.*

However he was then careful, in his longer and more prominent thoughts, to signal his content and that he had a desire to use the lavatory facilities.

'I must use the toilet,' he stated, jumping off the bed with a bound. 'Then I'll come back and cuddle you all.'

He would like to have made for the main door of the room into the corridor but the kids and his wife were all in the way.

If they are my kids and my wife and if this still is my hotel room.

He was not sure anymore and he locked the over-strong door of the lavatory very carefully and then taking the key out of the lock he looked through the keyhole. He could not see Sally and the girls in the room. All he could see were three huge creatures reminiscent of an impossible cross between an enormous sea anemone and a squid. They were standing in the hotel room with their tentacles waving in the air, waiting for him to come out of the bathroom. They had even started to sing in a surprisingly harmonious and enticing manner.

'Coming soon,' he announced loudly and as he looked the creatures flowed into the shape of his two daughters and his wife.

Oh sugar, he thought. *This has to be a dream.*

He pinched himself. It hurt and he did not wake up. He always woke up promptly from dreams as soon as he realised that he was dreaming.

If it's not a dream somebody has spiked my drinks.

But he had drunk bottled water at lunchtime and eaten some sandwiches that were freshly made in front of him.

The tea...it must have been the tea.

But he had used his own tea bag of green tea, one he carried with him on journeys, and fresh water from the tap.

If it's not hallucinogenic drugs then this is reality, he pondered. *And reality has recently been stretched by the clashing of worlds and shift in fundamental constants. But if they are not my wife and daughter what has happened to the real ones? Are Sally, Milly and Molly still alive?*

Chapter 14

'There's a very strange man coming towards the front door,' cried Molly, who was looking out of the front bedroom window with her sister.

'In what way is he strange, dear?' asked Sally.

'He just ate next door's dog,' replied the young girl. 'I saw him do it.'

'He can't have done,' answered Sally. 'You must be imagining things.'

'I saw it too,' said Milly. 'But I just couldn't believe it. so I didn't say anything. His head sort of caved in and then he swallowed the dog whole.'

'Then he turned back into a proper man,' added Molly.

There was a loud knock at the door.

Very strange things have been happening over the last few years, thought Sally. *So the kids might well be right. In which case there is no way I am going to open that door.*

'Quickly,' she said to the children. 'Follow me.'

She looked out of a back bedroom window and also saw someone very similar approaching from the rear of the house so she led the twins down the stairs and into the cellar, locking the door behind her.

'Keep very quiet,' she told the kids as they climbed down into the stygian darkness. 'If they are as weird as you say they'll probably break in and come looking for us but with a bit of luck they'll move on to another house and I will be able to call the police.'

They sat still for a few minutes and then heard noises within their house. Sally was inwardly cursing that she had not brought her mobile phone down with her. She had left it charging in the bedroom.

'OK,' she whispered. 'Here's the deal. While they are searching our house we will creep out through the coal hole but we must do it very quietly indeed. OK?'

The girls nodded very solemnly and Sally picked her way through the cellar rooms in the dark followed by Milly holding onto her mother's skirt and Molly holding on to Milly. Sally's heart was pounding so hard with fear that she was convinced the intruders could hear it and she could only wonder what the twins were experiencing.

Eventually, by carefully feeling their way, they reached their goal. The coal hole led out on the pavement and it was a long time since Sally had given it any thought at all. Despite pushing hard the metal lid did not initially want to move then it gave suddenly, with a loud clatter. They all froze in horror but the noise did not appear to have disturbed the intruders.

Sally picked first Molly and then Milly and pushed them out of the hole into the bright sunshine of the Plymouth street. She then hauled herself through the hole and they ran off down the road looking for a place to hide and call for help.

*

Kurt shouted to the weird creatures telling them he would be a few moments more and then telephoned the police on his cellphone.

'I'm trapped in a hotel bathroom with three strange shape-changing creatures trying to get at me,' he whispered into the phone. 'They look a bit like giant squids or perhaps some form of octopus?'

'Oh yes sir,' replied the policeman. 'And my uncle is the man in the moon. Now stop wasting my time or I'll trace the call and have you arrested.'

'Please do,' whispered Kurt. 'I am one hundred per cent

serious about this. This is the name of my hotel and I'll now describe the monsters to you.'

Whilst Kurt was telling the man the name of his hotel the policeman checked the number Kurt was calling from and found that it tallied. Despite not being the brightest button in the Bristol force the policeman began to take notice and believe Kurt. At the very least, the policeman reasoned, the caller had to be psychotic...he was not simply a hoaxer. Moreover they had just received a notice from a Detective Superintendent telling everybody to be on the look-out for shape-changing monsters and here was someone reporting one.

As soon as Kurt finished the call the policeman rang the number that was on the emergency notice.

'Penny Graves here,' came the reply.

'Ma'am,' the policeman was suddenly nervous about making the report, it seemed so ridiculous. 'I don't quite know whether this is what you are looking for but I have just received a call from a very disturbed man here in Bristol who tells me that shape-changing monsters have trapped him in a hotel bathroom.'

'Give me all the details and I'll send a car round immediately,' replied Graves.

Moments later she was on the radio to Chief Inspector Williams.

'Daniel?'

'Yes ma'am.'

'There is a report of a shape-changing monster or maybe several in a hotel at the bottom of Pembroke Road in Bristol. Can you go there immediately?'

'I've not dropped Hercules and the sprite yet,' replied Williams. 'But I can go to Pembroke Road straight away if you don't mind me taking them along for the ride.'

'Take them,' ordered Graves. 'But get a move on. The caller was trapped in a bathroom and I don't think a bath sponge, a toilet roll and a bar of soap will hold the monsters off for very much longer.'

Dan Williams turned his car round and drove rapidly towards Clifton, cursing the twenty mile per hour limit and trebling it.

The limit was brought in to reduce car emissions and all it has done is increase them, thought Dan as he swerved past another irritating, almost stationary car that was sticking to the limit. *Which is exactly what they should have realised it would do given that the cars are now driving round in lower, less efficient gears and doing so for longer.*

In an annoyingly persistent computerised female voice his own car was telling him that he was exceeding the limit and that his misdemeanour would be logged.

You do that, thought Dan. *At least I'm the one in charge of the driving.*

Bristol had pioneered the use of driverless cars and if they had been in one of those there is no way he could have gone past any of the slow vehicles.

Dan pulled up outside the hotel leaving the car on double yellow lines, the car informing him yet again that his transgression had been recorded.

Sneak and turncoat, thought Dan as he jumped out, beckoning the other two to follow him as he did so.

'Let's see if we can catch a shape-changer,' said Williams with a grin, taking a package out of his pocket as he did so. 'And we'd better wear some of Johnsons' earplugs to prevent them from charming us.'

They ran into the reception area, demanded the room key and then bounded up the stairs to the room. The door was ajar when they got there and the bedroom was empty apart from the furniture and a patch of wet carpet centrally which Williams knelt down and sniffed.

'Don't touch that!' he warned Hercules and Lah Lah. 'It might be important evidence.'

The big policeman then walked over to the bathroom and tried the door. It was locked. Williams banged on the door.

'Open up, This is the police,' he demanded.

'How do I know that you are the police and not another shape-changing monster?' whispered Kurt in a querulous voice.

'Sorry,' replied Williams. 'I can't hear you too well.'

The policeman was reluctant to remove the earplugs in case the monsters returned.

'How do I know that you are the police?' shouted Kurt.

Williams pulled his identity card out of his pocket.

This is probably a paranoid nutter who has had a psychotic episode and wet himself, he thought as he held the card up in front of the keyhole.

'Thank god you are here,' burbled Kurt as he opened the door. 'Have the monsters gone?'

'Yes,' replied Williams drily, then he muttered. 'If there ever were any monsters.'

'Oh!' exclaimed Kurt. 'I don't think you really believe that they were here or that they trapped me in the bathroom. Have a look at the footage I took of them on my phone. There's only a small range of view because I took the pictures through the keyhole but I think you will see enough to be convinced.'

His smart phone had a projection facility built-in so Kurt projected the footage on the wall. Hercules, as fascinated as the others, went to sit down and found himself falling to the floor.

'Wasn't there a big armchair just here, to the right of the door?' asked Hercules.

'No,' replied Kurt.

'Yes,' answered Williams and Lah Lah.

'It was covered in a chintzy, floral pattern material,' added the sprite. 'It was a pattern I hadn't seen before which didn't really suit the room.'

'There was no armchair there,' stated Kurt.

'Oh lord!' cried Williams. 'The shape-changers were in the room the whole time and we didn't see them. They were disguised as an armchair and they've escaped while we were concentrating on your phone footage. Quick, into the corridor.'

They ran out into the hotel corridor, tapping a drinks machine as they skirted past it to check that it was real.

The reception lobby was deserted and the receptionist had disappeared. Where she had been standing there was just another patch of wet carpet.

'I think that my wife and children are in danger,' cried Kurt, suddenly recalling his fears. 'The monsters imitated them.'

Kurt gave Williams all the details and the big policeman telephoned through to friends at the Plymouth HQ.

'They'll pop round to your place in Plymouth straight away,' stated the detective chief inspector. 'So try not to worry.'

'If they're targeting relatives and friends of the missing professionals they may well go for Passmore as well,' growled Hercules.

'You're right,' agreed Williams. 'We'd better go round and pick him up. His house is very near here.'

Williams phoned Penny Graves hands-free whilst taking the short trip round to Passmore's house and she agreed that they needed to reconvene immediately.

'With this new footage and an eyewitness we are into a different ballgame,' she added. 'And we seem to be in need of a marine biologist.'

'We're in luck there,' grunted Williams. 'That's exactly what Kurt Collins does for a living.'

∗

Sally and the twins were hiding in a neighbour's house a couple of hundred yards down the road. The owner had reluctantly let them in as he didn't know them very well having only met them at a street party. Sally had to explain the situation several times before he would allow her to use the telephone. She eventually reached the duty desk of the main Plymouth police station.

'Some sort of monster swallowed a dog whole and then broke into my house,' she explained.

'Are you sure that it wasn't a bulhaggle that scared your children,' replied the sergeant on the desk.

'Certainly not,' replied Sally. 'There are no scarecrows in our street. We are in the middle of town.'

'Wait a minute,' said the sergeant. 'What did you say your name was?'

'It was and still is Dr. Sally Collins,' stated Sally.

'Now don't get tilby with me, young lady,' replied the policeman. 'I think I have just had an enquiry about you.'

The policeman shouted for the inspector to be informed that a Sally Collins was on the line. The inspector came bounding down and took the call.

'Hello Dr. Collins. This is Inspector Roobottom. You don't know me but we've just received a call about your husband. He's OK but wants us to check on you.'

Sally explained the situation and the inspector agreed to send a car immediately. She could hear the duty sergeant grumbling in the background as she put the phone down ....he was saying something about hoax calls and the inspector was putting him right.

*

Dan Williams, Hercules, Lah Lah and Kurt Collins arrived at Rick Passmore's house within fifteen minutes. They stood knocking at the door and eventually a dripping wet University Reader opened the door to them, dressed only in a towel.

'How can I help you?' the tall, handsome man asked Williams. 'Have there been developments?'

'There have but may I ask you why you are so wet?' the detective chief inspector was intrigued and suspicious.

'I have a swimming pool in the basement,' replied Dr. Passmore. 'Would you like to see it? Come in, come in.'

'The guys searched your house when Dame Foxleigh went missing,' commented Dan. 'But they didn't tell me that you had a pool.'

'They were probably not that impressed,' replied Passmore. 'I understand that pools like mine are commonplace in London.'

'I wouldn't say commonplace,' remarked Dan. 'But there are quite a few.... and basements with gymnasia, movie theatres, bowling alleys.'

'Well, this is just a little pool. What do you think fellers?'

Passmore threw open the door to the pool room.

The pool stretched from the front of the house to the back, perhaps twenty-eight or thirty feet in length and fourteen feet across. It was a beautiful green colour with subtle underwater lighting and complex patterns on its floor and sides. However, more striking than this were the plants around the pool. Kurt looked up to the ceiling. Sure enough there were UV lights... there had to be or the plants would not have survived. He noted the biggest Monstera deliciosa, or Swiss cheese plant, that he had ever seen and it was bearing fruit like a big green corn on the cob. There was a passion flower in full bloom, several rubber plants, a fruiting orange tree, an enormous flowering amaryllis standing in a pot, a number of palms and a large, black domestic cat that stalked away in typical feline disdain when they looked at it. The overall effect was incredible....the place looked like a natural pool in the middle of a remote jungle.

'You like it don't you?' asked Passmore.

'I do,' agreed Williams. 'It's like a slice of paradise. But we must get back to the police station.'

'Won't be a moment,' grinned the likable scientist. 'My

clothes are just in this small changing room.'

The man disappeared into the room and appeared a few moments later fully clothed. The speed was so great that Williams was amazed.

'Practice,' Passmore winked at Williams. 'I swim everyday and I'm always jumping in and out of my clothes.'

*

The neighbour in Plymouth was beginning to warm to the twins. Sally did not find that surprising since in her eyes they could do no wrong but they were certainly charming the man. When the police arrived the lonely man was even quite sorry to see them go.

'You will come back and visit to tell me what happens?' he asked wistfully.

'We'd loved too,' they chorussed back at him.

I'm sure they would, thought Sally. *It was the chocolate biscuits that did the trick.*

'We'd like to cruise past your house to see if there is any activity now,' stated the driver of the vehicle.

Sally had asked to see their identity cards. She was taking no more chances.

The police car drove along the couple of hundred yards to the house and then stopped. Lights could be seen going on and off around the Collins' home.

'Should there be anybody in there right now?' asked the driver.

'No-one,' replied Sally. 'There's just me, the twins and Kurt.'

'And where is Kurt?' asked the police driver. 'I presume that he is your husband?'

'He's in Bristol and your inspector actually spoke to him,' replied Sally. 'And yes, you are right, he is my husband.'

'And he's our daddy,' chorussed the twins.

'OK,' said the driver. 'So the conclusion is that the intruders are still in the house. I shall go and arrest them.'

'Don't do that,' cried the twins in tandem.

'Why not?' ask the policeman. 'They've broken into your house so they have broken the law. I can catch them red-handed.'

'They're not just people, like us,' said Molly in a wise voice.

'So what are they?' asked the policeman, slightly amused.

'They're monsters and they could easily eat you,' replied Milly.

*

'Has anyone seen or heard of a creature like this?' asked Penny Graves, looking around and thinking that the incident room was becoming a bit crowded.

'Similar but not identical,' remarked Kurt Collins.

'Go ahead,' replied Graves. 'The floor is yours.'

'Mimic octopuses, we marine biologists call them,' said Kurt

'Octopuses?' Passmore looked shocked. 'We're talking about octopuses at a time like this?'

Collins, surprised by the intervention, stopped talking.

'Please go on, Kurt,' implored Penny Graves. 'Dr. Passmore is upset because he has lost a friend but let me assure you that we do want to hear what you have to say.'

'Well the Mimic octopuses are just one example of marine creatures that can use camouflage, movement and shape-changing to actively, and very successfully mimic other sea life,' said Kurt Collins.

'So they are shape-changers?' asked Jim Rogers.

'Yes and without the use of magic,' nodded the marine biologist. 'Imagine what they could do if they could also use hexes and spells.'

'What are they able to look like?' asked Dan Williams.

'A variety of other creatures such as venomous sea snakes or lionfish. But I don't want to get bogged down in this detail,' Kurt Collins waved a hand. 'The octopus was just an example to persuade you that sea animals exist that can shape-change.'

'Before we leave the octopus could you tell us what other animals it can look like?' asked DS Johnson. 'I had no idea that an octopus could do this.'

'As well as sea snakes and lionfish it can look like flatfish, giant crabs, seashells, stingrays, jellyfish and a whole load of weird creatures that may or may not have an earthly existence,' replied Collins looking at Johnson. 'If you are really interested you can read about them on the internet or speak to the aquarist at the excellent Bristol Aquarium.'

'And you think that these creatures are similar?' asked Jim Rogers.

'Functionally, yes,' replied Collins. 'Although they look more like an impossible cross between a squid and a sea anemone.'

'Hercules,' stated Penny Graves. 'You look as if you have something to add.'

'I do,' stated the booming voice of Hercules. 'But I'm not quite sure about its relevance.'

'Spit it out,' ordered Penny Graves. 'Come on.'

'I'm extremely old,' stated Hercules. 'Over four thousand years old.'

'Go on,' urged Penny, secretly pushing down her disbelief. Since the cataclysm equally old supernatural creatures had appeared so she had to accept the reality of the Greek demigod.

'And when I was young I heard tell of creatures much like this,' added Hercules.

'And what were they?' asked Penny.

'Long ago, when I was young, seafarers were a rarer and wilder breed. They talked of such things as sirens and mermaids. Creatures that lured fishermen to their doom.'

The ancient Greek legend's voice filled the room as he spoke.

'And do you think that these creatures existed?' asked Penny.

'Yes I do,' replied the great hero, looking very pensive. 'They were a problem to Jason and the Argonauts and very similar creatures, river nymphs, stole my servant and drowned him.'

'Have you seen these monsters since that time?' asked Penny, astounded by what she was hearing.

'No, probably not,' conceded Hercules. 'But I have long considered that they were unlikely to have been mammalian.'

'So what are they?' asked Williams, horrified at the thought.

'Maybe something like the octopus Dr. Collins referred to or some kind of fish, perhaps, or even a reptile. But their abilities were enhanced by charm, which is a form of magic and there has, until recently, been a dearth of charm on Earth.'

'Shape-changing lizards ruling the world?' cried Passmore scornfully. 'You'll be invoking the shade of David Icke next. That's where you are going with this one. It's ridiculous and it's not helping us to find the culprit.'

'There must be more than one culprit Dr. Passmore,' countered Penny Graves. 'And I'm not sure that you are right to say that Hercules was suggesting shape-changing lizards were ruling the world.'

'No, I wasn't,' agreed Hercules. 'But if the sirens have somehow overcome their need to be in the water and have managed to exist on dry land then they could, perhaps, be behind these attacks.'

'I thought the sirens were girls,' said Sid Johnson. 'Or am I remembering the myths incorrectly?'

'Most of them were female,' agreed Hercules. 'But tradition tells us that their father was Achelous, the most senior river god.... and I expect that there were a few male sirens.'

'There don't really need to be if they can shape change,' muttered Williams. 'They could be any sex or none.'

'This is ridiculous,' gasped Passmore. 'I was happy to suggest magic was involved but sirens? That's surely beyond possibility. I thought that the culprit must come from Faerie as they all have done before. Surely it is well known that the fairies spirit people away and they are never found.'

'I do have to take issue with that remark,' said Peter Mingan, the werewolf. 'Not all of the problems have come from Faerie. It is true that Parsifal X had a hand in creating the clashing of realities but Dagon the money god was from Earth, Lucifer is from the Eternal Realm.'

'Let's not go into arguments about the past and which reality is to blame,' suggested Penny Graves. 'And we will replay that little piece of video from Foxleigh's camera. Perhaps, Dr. Passmore, you should go out if it is going to upset you again?'

'I'll be fine,' said the tall, elegant scientist.

'I would particularly like you all to look at the lips of Foxleigh's attacker at the beginning of the sequence.'

So saying Penny put the part in question on a loop.

'Now we don't have any sound...it didn't record for some reason. But we have had our lip readers do a quick job on it and they came up with the following. *I am Acker Low Us*. Is that the same name as you suggested for the river god?'

Hercules was surprised and nodded his head vehemently.

'Yes, yes. So the old man of the river has survived all this time,' the famous hero looked impressed. 'It's bad luck he is on the wrong side.'

'So it is the name of the sirens' father?' Penny wanted to be certain.

'Yes,' agreed Hercules. 'He didn't look like that when I knew him but he also has charm and shape-changing abilities.'

'DCI Williams, you have had a runaround with Sergeant Johnson and brought Hercules to this meeting along with Lah Lah the sprite. Do you have anything to add to the discussion?'

'I think I do,' said the big man. 'The CEO of the penal hospital in Princetown had persuasive abilities or charm exactly as you described.'

'As does the man Dick or Peter Whittington,' chipped in Lah

Lah. 'They are both probably sirens. We found that the best way to combat the charm was by the use of earplugs.'

'That's an interesting suggestion but the next question is what do we do about all of this?' stated Penny Graves, writing on a computer tablet and the scribblings appearing on the big screen. 'We don't know why the scientists are being targeted and we have not yet identified a common theme. Until we can do that we will not be able to predict where the sirens are or who they will go for next. We have a lot of conjecture and not much information. So let us all have a short break then we should get back to work making suggestions which Jim Rogers can try out on the POIROT network. Sergeant Johnson would you mind ordering some take-away food? I can see that this is going to take all evening and maybe into the night.'

Chapter 15

-*This is Alpha Foxtrot One over*
-*We copy you*
-*I need some back up with firepower at the Plymouth address please, this is a code Indigo alert. I repeat code Indigo*

'What does code indigo mean?' asked Molly.

'It means that magic is involved,' answered the policeman.

'So why don't you just say magic?' asked Milly. 'It's silly to say code indigo when you could just say magic.'

'Fine, kids,' replied the policeman. 'Can you just leave this to me?'

'Shush children,' ordered their Mum. 'The poor man is trying to work.'

'Why is he poor, mum?' asked Molly. 'He doesn't look poor.'

'Quiet now,' replied Sally. 'Pipe down and we'll watch what happens.'

The waiting dragged on and finally the driver became too impatient.

'I'm going in,' he declared. 'Are you going to come with me?'

The question was directed to his team-mate who nodded in reply then spoke.

'I'll go to the door to back you up.'

'Have you got a gun? asked Molly fearfully. 'Because you'll have to shoot the monsters.'

'I've got a taser,' replied the policeman. 'So I'll be fine.'

*

When the food arrived at the Bristol incident room the assembled company were still busy and they continued to plan as they ate.

'So we should get a squad to raid the Bedlam hospital and pick up the CEO,' said DCI Rogers as he munched on a sandwich.

'And also find Peter Whittington or Dick as he persuaded us to call him,' added Hercules. 'I would be happy to join that detail. I have a score to settle with him.'

'You've searched for water connections before, haven't you?' Kurt Collins asked Jim Rogers as the policeman sat at the large computer screen.

'By occupation and place, yes,' agreed Rogers. 'The results were not significantly different from the same search on random professionals who are not missing.'

'Did you add hobbies and pastimes such as fishing and sailing?' asked Collins. 'And any special requirements for a large water supply, such as power generation?'

'I'll add those,' agreed Rogers. 'Any other suggestions?'

'Sewage disposal,' replied Kurt. 'That's always contentious.'

Rogers spent a few more minutes entering the requests and suddenly the POIROT program spat out a result... a correlation of 0.9.

'That's amazing,' commented Jim Rogers. 'Look, if I compare it with the same search on random professionals the figure is 0.1. I think we've cracked it.'

He then did severally layered correlation and honed the results further.

'Everybody,' Rogers announced. 'I think we have an important result. All bar one or two of the professionals had a significant connection with the sea or a major river system either by work of hobby. The most vulnerable people are those most intimately connected with the sea and rivers....maritime experts, marine biologists, fish farmers, sewage disposal, people who work in industries which discharge waste into the rivers. Then come hobbies such as angling or sailing.'

'We'll send warnings to the conferences,' proposed Penny Graves.

'It's bigger than that,' grimaced Rogers. 'Having identified the targets we can now see that many more of the missing people have disappeared for the same reason.'

'How can you be sure that they are all part of the same problem?' asked Passmore. 'Maybe it really is just coincidence.'

'I'm pretty certain the correlation is solid,' argued Rogers.

'What about Dr. Alan Malova, the neurologist?' asked Dan Williams. 'How does he relate to rivers or seas?'

'His research was heavily involved in the use of the giant squid nerve axon,' replied Rogers. 'Kurt could explain more about that since his work was in the same field.'

'Not actually my work but, yes, my professor has been researching into nerve conduction using the giant squid. The scientists use the nerves from the giant squid because the axon is so large and they can actually measure the potential difference using electrodes.'

'Not your work?' Rick Passmore raised his eyebrows. 'I thought that was exactly your field!'

'Not at all,' answered Kurt. 'I'm an expert on algae and my wife, Sally, works with hermit crabs. The professor asked me to deliver her lecture at the conference here in Bristol but I added some environmental issues from Sally's work and my own.'

'So the neurologist also worked with a maritime connection?' asked Penny, seeking clarification.

'Seems like it,' agreed Rogers. 'Add to that the fact that all of these strange disappearances have occurred within spitting distance of rivers or seas and it becomes a tragedy of epidemic proportion.'

'Kurt, as a marine biologist who has actually seen these creatures is there anything more you can add?' asked Penny Graves.

'Only to say that the creatures did look maritime in nature and if that is the case even if they are using magic to enable them to survive on dry land they will need to get back to the sea or river eventually.'

'How long would you think they could survive out of water?' asked DCI Williams.

'This is just a guess but I would say only a few hours at the most,' answered the biologist.

'What are you basing that guess on?' asked Passmore. 'It sounds rather random.'

'Well I'm assuming they are cephalopods. An octopus can climb out of water for a matter of minutes only,' answered Kurt. 'Another possibility based on the strange appearance is anemones. I would consider that much less likely as these creatures are clearly intelligent and anemones are not.'

'Would it alter your estimate of the time they can stay out of water?' asked Penny Graves.

'Anemones vary enormously,' Kurt scratched his head as he replied. 'And they may be intertidal or in rock pools, in which case they may have to survive up to several hours whilst the pool dries up until the tide comes in again. So yes, an anemone might stay out of water much longer but I'm betting that they were originally cephalopods not anemones.'

'You mentioned squids earlier. How do they fare out of water?' asked Jim Rogers.

'They do worse than the octopus but don't read too much into my figure,' replied Kurt. 'This is a new species to science and it might have considerably greater tolerance to time away from H_2O.'

'The fact that the attacks occur near rivers and seas....does that influence your thoughts on the matter?' prompted Penny Graves.

'Of course,' replied Kurt. 'But there is something else. When the three monsters in my hotel room were surprised by Chief

Inspector Williams supported by Hercules and Lah Lah they hid jointly as a large armchair. But they left behind a pool of water.'

'Now why is that significant?' asked Graves.

'They were presumably warned by somebody at the front desk but had nowhere to go so they were shocked and had to change quickly,' said Kurt. 'In that situation the control of their water, which must be needed for survival, was imperfect.'

'There was another puddle down by the front desk,' Williams reminded everybody. 'So the receptionist was also a shape-changer and had to do an emergency morphing.'

'Or another shape-changer swallowed the receptionist while we were in the hotel room,' suggested Lah Lah. 'And lost water while doing so.'

'This is all very useful,' said Penny Graves. 'I shall put round a further notice to all units around the country and inform Interpol.'

'But we'll never catch them or stop them unless we can control their leader,' stated Hercules.

'How do you intend doing that?' asked Passmore. 'The creature must be highly intelligent to have survived all these years and to have avoided capture.'

'Although they are shape-changers they are not miracle workers,' reasoned Hercules. 'In the case of your friend Marianne Foxleigh the creature managed to imitate you almost perfectly and if you had not had a cast-iron alibi you would still be in the frame.'

'True,' agreed Passmore with a smile. 'But I don't see where this is getting us.'

'The monster must have spent some time observing you and Foxleigh so it is likely to be someone close to you or to have taken the place of someone close.'

'Or simply to have posed as an armchair,' added Passmore.

'And they can read minds to a rudimentary extent,' threw in

Kurt. 'I observed this when they were targeting me.'

'What exactly do you mean when you say "to a rudimentary extent"?' asked Penny Graves.

'They could read the thoughts I projected as my main subvocalisation,' explained Kurt. 'But they could not read my intentions.'

'That may only be some of them,' suggested Passmore. 'Maybe the river god himself is highly intelligent and able to read much deeper thoughts.'

'All these things are possible,' agreed Penny Graves. 'But we really won't know until we catch one.'

'Which doesn't seem very likely at the moment,' Passmore sounded depressed again.

'True,' agreed Williams, the feeling of depression wafting over him.

'Unless, perhaps, we catch Dick Whittington or the CEO of Bedlam,' cried the ever cheerful Hercules. 'I'm game for trying!'

'God you're a tonic for a dying man,' Williams clapped Hercules on the shoulder. 'Why don't you join our force permanently?'

'Maybe I'll do just that,' smiled the gigantic superhero. 'Maybe I will.'

*

The police driver and his companion returned from the Collins' house about ten minutes later and the driver put the car into gear and set off without as much as a single word spoken.

'How did you get on?' asked Sally, leaning forward from her position in the back of the car.

'Sit back,' replied the driver curtly.

'But did you find the intruders?' asked Sally as she sat back, obeying the command.

'What's done is done,' replied the other policeman.

'Where are we going now?' asked Molly.

'Do you want us to make a statement?' asked Milly.

'I'm driving,' muttered the police driver.

Sally and the twins sat back glumly. The driver was using a mobile phone, holding it illegally against his ear and muttering away and they did not even appear to be driving towards the police station.

'I would like to know where we are going,' Sally repeated Molly's question very evenly and politely

'We're taking you down to the river,' said the companion policeman. 'Do you have a problem with that?'

The reply was so menacing that Sally shut up completely.

*

'We've just received a phone call,' announced Jim Rogers to the group in the incident room. 'I've discussed it with Superintendent Graves and she has told me to make it public to all of us here.'

'What did the caller say?' asked DCI Williams.

'The caller identified himself as a son of the river and sea,' replied Rogers. 'And he pointed out that he knew how much we valued our elvers.'

'Did you ask him if he meant offspring?' asked Williams.

'Straight away and he agreed that was indeed what he meant,' added Rogers. 'He then said that the offspring and the maternal unit would not be harmed if we stopped our investigations.'

'Did he say what their names were?' asked Williams.

'Not as yet but he is going to come back to me on that one,' replied Rogers.

Kurt exchanged worried looks with Dan Williams.

'I will telephone Plymouth HQ and check that your family are safe,' Williams said to Kurt.

'I've still not been able to get them on the phone,' replied the marine biologist. 'So I am very disturbed.'

Rogers' telephone rang.

'OK,' he replied to the caller and tapped a button on his computer as he did so. 'I understand and we will suspend operations and send out a notice cancelling the warnings. That's right. That will happen as of now. But you are sure of your prisoners' identities? Fine. Do you wish to speak to anyone here. No? OK. You'll come back to me with your future demands, I understand. When you do come back to us you say we will have six hours to respond. Could you make that eight? You can't? OK. Are you sure that you don't want to speak to anyone here. Oh ....He's just cut the call.'

Rogers put his mobile down.

'I'm not sure that the offspring of the river god are as bright as the original god himself,' said Rogers, typing coordinates into his computer as he spoke.

'Why do you say that?' asked Sid Johnson.

'They let me talk them into staying online long enough for me to trace exactly where they are,' replied Rogers. 'And Dr. Collins sit down please. It definitely is your wife and kids that they are holding.'

Kurt looked completely distraught and Lah Lah tried to comfort him.

'Alternatively they may be as bright but rather naive and poorly educated,' suggested Sid Johnson, replying to Rogers' implication that the shape-changers were stupid.

'Which is highly likely if they have only recently been able to stay away from water for any length of time,' surmised Penny Graves. 'And if that is the case it is important that we stop this sooner rather than later as they will inevitably become more intelligent and better educated.'

'So where are my twins and my Sally?' asked Kurt, cutting through the banter.

'They have been taken to the National Marine Aquarium in Plymouth,' answered Jim Rogers.

'What a strange place to take someone,' remarked Hercules.

'Not if you are a sea creature but wish to remain on dry land,' countered Rogers. 'They have the country's biggest aquarium there. The sirens could pop in and out of the tanks whenever they wished and be ready to masquerade as men or women.'

'And children,' groaned Kurt. 'They can also pretend that they are children.'

They all looked at Kurt in dismay.

'What are we going to do about my children?' he asked.

'I've sent a posse from Plymouth,' admitted Rogers. 'But you should be quite reassured that they are in good spirits.'

'How do you figure that out?' asked Kurt, to whom the news seemed relentlessly bad.

'They did say they had your wife, Polly Collins, and two girls. I asked for the girls names and the spokesman replied that they were Mickey Mouse and Donald Duck. The girls had told him themselves. I presume that they are not the names of your girls?'

'Their real names are Milly and Molly,' replied the marine biologist, trying hard to remain calm.

'So the shape-changers are not necessarily au fait with our culture,' remarked Passmore, who had just returned from the lavatory and had apparently missed a minute or two of the conversation. 'But that doesn't necessarily make them stupid.'

'That's just what Sid thinks,' nodded Jim Rogers. 'And I've suggested that the original river god is intelligent and better educated than his children.'

'Do you really think so?' asked Passmore

'I'm certain that he is,' answered Rogers. 'He has survived a very long time and he fooled one of the brightest scientists we had in Britain.'

'If you mean my dear Marianne,' countered Passmore. 'She was very good at manipulating the media but not so good with the data. Though I loved her dearly she wasn't that intelligent.'

'But she was a Dame for her services to science,' protested Rogers.

'Truly so,' agreed Passmore with a mischievous grin. 'And she was very proud of it!'

'Rightly so I expect,' Penny Graves bristled slightly. It annoyed her when people made suggestions to the effect that women did not deserve high honours.

'True, true,' agreed Rick Passmore, smiling benignly. 'But I missed what started this conversation. Apart from the erroneous names why was the suggestion made that the shape-changers are daft?'

'They stayed on the phone long enough for us to trace their position,' replied Penny Graves.

'Yes,' pondered Passmore. 'I can see that does indeed make them appear daffy.'

'Not so daft as we think,' replied Rogers who was again replying to a phone call. 'When the police got to the Aquarium the place was blazing with lights, nobody was around and there was just a single mobile phone in the middle of the floor.'

'Did they touch it?' asked Williams.

'Was it booby trapped?' asked Penny Graves almost simultaneously.

'They picked it up and it was not booby-trapped,' replied Rogers.

'They were lucky,' Graves was deadly serious.

'And the device rang immediately,' said Rogers, holding his hand over the mouthpiece of the phone. 'The shape-changers were on the line and said that we have shown duplicity. Clearly we have not called off the hunt for them and they stressed that they are not stupid and the girls real names are Milly and Molly. They also said that they would be in touch soon to make their final demands which will have increased and we will not be given as much time.'

'That puts us in our place,' sighed Sid Johnson.

Penny Graves got up and walked around for a few minutes. She looked out of the window, down the corridor and into the other adjacent offices.

'It does something more than that,' she said. 'I want every one to place their mobile phones on the table.'

A plethora of phones appeared.

'Now,' said Penny. 'We are a team and we are all prepared for what I am going to say and there will be no leaks to the media or whatever. What is more we are ready if any of us are contacted by the shape-changers.'

'What are you going to suggest?' asked Passmore.

'I do not think that this ongoing campaign by the shape-changers is a random event,' stated Penny. 'I've listened to all of the happenings and I've been trying to put this together into a whole.'

They all looked at the Detective Superintendent attentively. What was she going to say? Where was this leading?

'If we take it chronologically we must start with Hercules.'

The huge Greek hero stirred in his chair.

'He was disabled by magical spells five years ago at the same time as Parsifal X attacked Earth. I have it on good authority that other powerful supernatural entities that were resident on Earth were all assaulted at the same time.'

'Were there any?' asked Dan Williams. 'We certainly weren't aware of their presence.'

'They have been very subtle over the years and managed to hide from view but we do know about some of them. But probably not all,' Penny stressed the last sentence.

'Which ones should we know about?' asked Jim Rogers.

'Most obviously there was the Scott family,' Penny looked round and the team were nodding their heads. 'Jimmy Scott's mother-in-law was a very powerful witch, Jimmy and his family are all archangels. Parsifal X endeavoured to maroon them on a small island and then sent avatars to kill them.'

'OK,' agreed Rogers. 'We do know about them it is true.'

'Then we have Count Dracula,' stated Penny Graves.

'Dracula?' Dan Williams expressed everybody's amazement.

'This must stay in this room but, yes, Dracula,' replied Graves.

'Does such a person exist?' asked Williams.

'He does and he has been very useful to us over the last few months. Voluntarily on his part and entirely in secret,' replied Graves.

'We are talking about vampires, blood-sucking, impaling etcetera?' asked Williams.

'Correct.'

'Then how come we don't know about it?' asked Jim Rogers.

'The decision was made to keep this at a very high level,' replied Graves. 'I was the lowest level permitted to know.'

'So what happened to him?' asked Rogers.

'He was attacked by a couple of powerful spell wielders from Faerie, originally at the behest of Parsifal X,' answered Graves.

'Is he still alive?' asked Passmore, his eyebrows raised in surprise.

'Parsifal X or Dracula,' queried Graves, standing tall and cool, the example of a modern policewoman.

'Count Dracula,' disambiguated Passmore.

'Yes and he's very charming, in fact,' replied Graves, blushing minimally.

'But how does this relate to our present situation?' asked Passmore.

'I'm actually getting to that,' countered Graves, just slightly irritated with Passmore's impatience despite the man's obvious charm. 'The two spell wielders who disabled Dracula were offered important concessions by X. In fact one was offered dominion over the entire world.'

'Any other powerful creatures captured in the last few years?' asked Williams.

'Of course,' continued Graves. 'I would not be able to make a case from just the Scotts and Dracula. A gorgon had survived until now and that also was captured by forces loyal to Parsifal X. Then we come to Hercules.'

Penny Graves turned and looked at Hercules, as did everybody else in the room.

'If what we hear is to be believed Hercules is a demigod,' Penny stared at the huge figure and he just shrugged his shoulders. 'For five years he has thought that he was someone called Tim Cranbrook and that he had been paralysed in an industrial magic accident.'

The team continued to stare at the massive man, seven foot of muscle and power.

'That's true,' nodded Hercules. 'That is what I thought.'

'And we believe it was a spell-wielding person of immense power who kept him that way,' continued Penny. 'Once again this will have been to disarm this hero, this protector of the planet Earth.'

'I don't see how Count Dracula fits into this. He's hardly a protector of Earth,' stated Rogers.

'His attitude has changed over the years,' replied Penny. 'And Parsifal X was trying to contain and neutralise any person or creature that could put up a resistance against him. But I'll move on. The real questions are these. Is Dick Whittington in league with the shape-changers? Was the CEO of Bedlam in league with them also? Are they both shape-changers? Where is the monster who attacked and presumably killed Dame Marianne Foxleigh? Is he really the chief of all the shape-changers and what was the deal Parsifal X made with him?'

'Penny,' Rick Passmore spoke first, 'This is all very well but it is just conjecture. What makes you think that this monster we are talking about actually did go into a deal with Parsifal X?'

'That's a good question and really gets to the nub of my argument,' replied Penny. 'The evidence is coincidental and circumstantial but rather convincing. I am relying very much on the timing.'

Passmore nodded as if he understood then spoke again.

'I agree that Hercules was put out of action at a very convenient time for Parsifal X but why do you not think that the so-called river god did not just act on his own volition?'

'Because he could have acted at any time over the last four thousand years,' replied Penny. 'The river god and its offspring obviously retained considerable powers even before the clashing of the worlds. How else could another sentient species manage to hide from scientific scrutiny for so long?'

'Perhaps through their unique abilities as shape-changers and through charm,' replied Passmore.

'That's exactly what I am referring to,' answered Penny. 'They are the powers that have been retained.'

Passmore twisted his head as if to concede the point.

'But how could a river god have managed to best me in this way?' asked Hercules. 'I've fought worse before and managed to beat them and all we had to do to negate their charm was to wear something in our ears, something that distorted the timbre of their voice.'

'Perhaps you underestimated the intelligence and cunning of the river god?' suggested Passmore. 'From what you said he must have been around even longer than yourself.'

'That is true,' the big man conceded the point. 'I do suffer from arrogance. That is the way of all immortals...we come, in our hubris, to believe in our own legends.'

'What else do you remember about Achelous?' Penny Graves asked Hercules.

'He was a suitor for Deianeira when I was also seeking her

hand in marriage,' stated Hercules, searching back through his long distant memories. 'He was powerful, being able to take the shape of a rambling bull or a writhing snake and, of course, that of a man.'

'What happened?' asked Lah Lah.

'She chose me,' shrugged Hercules.

'Wasn't there more to it than that?' asked Graves, having frantically investigated the legends on Wikipedia after she had been told about the continued existence of Hercules. 'Didn't you actually fight over Deianeira?'

'Now you mention it I believe we did,' replied Hercules. 'I'm not trying to be purposely difficult but it was a long time ago and it is hard to remember. I seem to recall that we were fighting in a contest to decide who should win her hand and he turned into a bull. I pulled off one of his horns and he had to surrender.'

'He then had a job getting the horn back, according to the legends,' added Penny.

'Did he get it back?' asked Hercules. 'I didn't know that. I gave it to the Naiads and they turned it into the cornucopia.'

'So the prince of all river gods had good reason to hate you,' concluded Penny. 'And would have been happy to go into a liaison with Parsifal X to defeat you.'

'Maybe,' agreed Hercules reluctantly. 'But he came to the wedding happily enough.'

'Didn't Hercules kill his wife?' asked Sid Johnson. 'I think I read that at school.'

Hercules looked completely beaten.

'That was a different wife, Sid,' replied the hero with his head bowed. 'And Hera was the person who hexed me in order that I would do it. She has always hated me.'

'Does she still exist?' asked Lah Lah. 'Could she be behind all these mishaps?'

'She might still exist,' replied Hercules. 'But I've had no

problems from her for over two thousand years.'

'So it is most likely that Parsifal X utilised the latent grudge that Achelous had against Hercules,' stated Jim Rogers.

'I believe that he may have been offered something more than that,' suggested Penny Graves. 'And that he was given the extra power to make that happen.'

'What?' asked Rogers.

'As the foremost god of the rivers Achelous was also the god of pure, sweet drinking water,' remarked Penny. 'Don't think that I knew all this before this case started... this is all information readily available on the internet.'

'What could X have offered?' asked Williams.

'Human beings have been polluting and destroying rivers and seas for millennia,' stated Penny Graves 'But this has become vastly worse over the past two hundred years ever since the inception of the industrial revolution.'

'True, true,' nodded Rick Passmore.

'The world population had reached well over seven billion by 2014 and estimates suggested it would top eight billion by now,' continued Graves. 'Yet the very source of life, the freshwater in the rivers, was being poisoned by industry, polluted by farmers and dammed by governments.'

The assembled company all looked on glumly.

'Meanwhile people continued to cut down rain-forests, burn fossil fuels, acidify the seas and create floating islands of plastic waste,' Penny felt she was close to preaching, tantamount to proselytising. 'So you can almost understand a river god joining forces in a coalition with Parsifal X. I believe that X promised to decrease the population and control the excesses of the human race.'

She looked round the room studying all the faces in front of her.

'Maybe he also promised to stop the destruction of the

rivers, a noble enough cause,' Penny stopped for a few moments, gathering her breath and her thoughts then picked up her notes and continued again.

'So if, in addition to stopping our campaign against the shape-changers we were able to persuade them that we could be influential in saving the rivers maybe they would listen. In return the creatures would have to stop their campaign against scientists and industrialists, farmers and governments...the people they are blaming for destroying the supply of sweet water.'

'So you are suggesting that we fool the shape-changers by promising to save the rivers?' asked Passmore.

'No, no, no!' cried Penny. 'You're a scientist. You should understand that we can't go on the way we have been doing. Despite hating their techniques and the loss of life involved I have to admit that I really think I understand why the monsters are doing what they are doing.'

'In effect we have created our own monsters by our profligate ways?' suggested Williams.

'Dan has put it very simply and I believe that he is right. We must use our influence to change the world and save the rivers,' concluded Penny. She then sat down looking exhausted and spent.

'But we don't have the means to influence people in that way,' protested Rick Passmore. 'How can we deliver on our promises?'

'We can point out that the population has not reached eight billion,' suggested Sid Johnson.

'That is only because of the clash of realities which killed about two billion people,' sighed Penny. 'Rick is right. It is the weak point in our argument. How can we make good on our promises?'

'I know many of the world leaders,' replied Hercules and all the people in the room looked at him in amazement. Hercules looked somewhat abashed. 'Or at least I did before I was incarcerated in a nursing home.'

'When you say you know them, do you mean on speaking terms?' asked Jim Rogers.

'Sure,' stated the giant. 'I've been around a very long time and know how the system works. Or at least I did know. I've not yet had a chance to catch up.'

'I don't quite understand,' asked Passmore. 'If you were a fellow called Tim Cranbrook who was an inspector for the HSE how could you have got to know all of the heads of government?'

'I no longer believe that I ever was a man called Cranbrook. I don't know if he even existed,' replied the ancient hero.

'Oh yes, he definitely existed,' pointed out Williams. 'But we believe Cranbrook died five years ago after an accident unrelated to yourself.'

'So how did you know heads of government?' asked Passmore, pushing the point.

'My expertise was always in fighting,' answered Hercules. 'And I kept up to date with the latest developments. I've been a general in over forty different countries and more than a hundred different armies. I've been the field marshall in charge of several armies.'

'Give one example, just one,' demanded the tall scientist.

'I saved the Prussian army from defeat at Waterloo,' said Hercules. 'I helped defeat the British in the American War of Independence but I played a part in the victory of the British against the Germans at El Alamein in 1942. I was with Genghis Khan's undefeated army ..... '

'Fine, fine....' Penny Graves held up her hand. 'I think we all accept that you did know world leaders up until your capture....'

'My incarceration under a thralldom.......' interjected the huge hero.

'OK, incarceration. But the worry is that the leaders change. Who did you know in the UK?'

'Penny, I knew them all but in particular advised a guy called Darcy Macaroon.'

'He's gone,' stated Passmore. 'He has been voted out.'

'So who is in power now? asked Hercules. 'I expect that I've met him.'

'Don't worry about the UK,' Penny waved her hands in some exasperation. 'I can deal with that side. What other countries can you help us with?'

'Francoise De Lacrue of France, James Raymond Patterson of Canada, Paul Carpentier of Switzerland, Gordon Trevithick, Australia, Doctor Marcus Johns of Sweden, Boris Barinov of Russia,' Hercules reeled off the names without a pause for breath. 'Do you want more names?'

'A lot of those are no longer in power,' replied Passmore.

'I think Hercules has made his point,' Penny interrupted what seemed to be heading towards a major dispute. 'And although some have retired many are active still.'

'And the ones that have retired are still influential...even deadbeats like Darcy Macaroon have their followers,' remarked Williams.

'But do you have any means of communicating with them quickly?' asked Penny.

'I have their personal telephone numbers all in my head,' replied the demigod. 'I can list those for you as well if you like.'

Passmore was looking out of the window as if in despair of the way things were going.

'Rick, you still look unhappy,' Penny was trying to pull him back into the group effort.

'We're arguing whilst this poor man's wife and children are in danger,' answered the tall, handsome scientist.

'We are waiting for the abductors to get back in touch,' replied Penny. 'So in the meantime we are trying to get our act together so that we have something to offer them.'

'The only thing worth offering them is a total surrender of our activity against them,' suggested Passmore. 'I don't see that we are in any position to offer anything else. We are not in a position of strength.'

A general hubbub of noise greeted this suggestion, most people, including even Kurt Collins, disagreeing in principle but agreeing that it mighty be the only course open to them. A feeling of depression and failure pervaded the incident room.

'OK, that's enough,' Penny held up a hand. 'I want to hear from Kurt what he thinks of that proposition.'

'Not much, really,' replied the marine biologist, summoning his waning spirit. 'These creatures have been murdering folk all over the world for the last five years and we have only just begun to get a grip on the extent of their activity. Even though I totally love my wife and kids I don't think abject surrender will work or that it would be ethical. Perhaps we could agree to a ceasefire, no recriminations on either side and any prisoners they have taken to be released unharmed.'

'We can try that as a ploy. Any other ideas?' asked Graves.

Passmore looked disengaged again and the others just shook their weary heads.

'Then we wait,' concluded Penny.

Chapter 16

The atmosphere in the incident room was getting tense waiting for further contact from the kidnappers. Jim Rogers was in continuous contact with other police teams around England, South and North. The Plymouth team had not managed to trace the whereabouts of the abductors and the Collins family. The police car had been dumped near to the National Marine Aquarium in Plymouth and a large SUV had been stolen. That was now the object of a national search but its whereabouts had not been discovered. The original police crew of the police car had not been found either.

The Collins' house in Plymouth had been thoroughly searched and the only abnormal finding was a couple of patches of fetid water. Forensic crews were deployed to the hotel in Clifton and the Collins' house in Plymouth and would be reporting back to Penny's team in Bristol and London. Interpol were informed of the situation but all they could do was to put out alerts.

Two hours later the kidnappers were on the line and this was put on general hands-free and broadcast in the incident room.

'We know what you have been debating,' said the spokesperson from the shape-changing abductors, speaking in a very level voice with little inflection. 'And we still believe that you are lying to us. Your only hope of seeing the Collins family alive is to completely surrender. You must organise an emergency meeting of the world leaders and they must sign a binding agreement to stop the destruction of the rivers and seas. If this does not happen we will not only kill the woman and the two identical offspring we will also kill world leaders, imitate them and institute our reforms anyway.'

'It will be very difficult to do what you say,' Rogers replied. 'We can do our best but we cannot guarantee success.'

'Then it will be your loss. You have an idea of how many people we have removed but what you do not know is how many we have already replaced.'

'What do you mean?' asked Penny Graves.

'We do not randomly kill people,' stated the abductor. 'We like to absorb the knowledge of the people we kill then we can impersonate them in intricate detail and.....'

'So you have concentrated on scientists because you can absorb their knowledge? That's amazing,' interrupted Kurt. 'But you must realise that both my wife and myself are completely in tune with your thinking about the rivers and seas. There is no reason to hurt her or my children. It will just harm your cause.'

'We are completely aware of the fact that some scientists and environmental agitators are in agreement with us. That has not stopped the pollution from increasing and the despoilment of the environment from worsening.'

'We are trying to do something about it!' exclaimed Penny Graves, annoyed at the patronising tone of the speaker.

'Despite the start that Parsifal X gave in reducing population you have continued on the same tack,' replied the shape-changing spokesperson. 'The birthrate shot up after the cataclysms. You seem congenitally incapable of learning anything.'

'Public opinion is changing against waste, against pollution, against over-population,' stated Penny Graves.

'Too little, too late,' cried the shape-changer. 'By the time you put into effect any of the changes you are trying to make the rivers and seas will be irrevocably harmed. We live in the rivers and seas and we are being poisoned. This has to stop.'

'We managed to mend the hole in the ozone layer,' stated Rogers.

'Which you had created in the first place,' replied the

spokesperson. 'No, we have been watching you for some time and have been appalled at your behaviour. Unnecessary conflicts and wars, money worship to an obscene level, disgusting waste, massive obesity problems due to your own inability or lack of desire to curb your appetite. This all has to stop and we intend stopping it.'

'Even if we manage to meet all your demands how do we know that you will honour your side of the bargain and not continue with your campaign of abduction?' asked Graves

'Sedition and seduction, bribery and corruption,' replied the shape-changer. 'Those are the actions of human beings not us. But we do not try to abduct your people. We try to absorb them and replace them. Unfortunately not all of our actions are successful and the unsuccessful cases become a missing person. They are, of course, not wasted.'

'In what way are they not wasted?' asked Penny Graves, knowing that she would not like the answer.

'They are a very useful food stuff,' replied the shape-changer.

'We need time to think about this,' replied Penny Graves. 'You have set us a very hard problem.'

'You have three more hours then we will kill the Collins family and continue our campaign of absorption of your cleverest people.'

'Why do you consider them to be the cleverest?' asked Rogers. 'You don't appear to have targeted rocket scientists?'

'They know nothing about the rivers and seas so they are stupid,' replied the shape-changer. 'Now hurry. You have very little time to contact all the numbers of world leaders.'

'Which numbers?' asked Penny Graves.

'The numbers that Hercules has stored in his brain,' replied the spokesperson.

The line went dead and the assembled company sat in stunned silence.

*

'Can I have a word with you in private?' Williams asked Penny Graves when there was a pause from the frantic attempts at contacting people. With the help of Hercules the police team had been trying to phone the various leaders of the former United Kingdom. Penny Graves considered that they needed permission from the UK leaders before they contacted the presidents, kings, despots and prime ministers that Hercules knew on a personal level. Due to the late hour it was proving difficult to reach anybody in authority.

'Certainly,' agreed Graves, responding to Williams' request. 'We shall step outside for a minute.'

She took the set of keys out of her pocket and opened the door into the corridor.

Kurt watched them go with some trepidation. Were they plotting a deal to save his family or would they sell him out? He did not know them very well but had trusted them to help him and his kinsfolk. At every turn the shape-changers had managed to outwit the police and to stay ahead of the team investigating them and here he sat whilst his wife and two children were in grave danger.

Penny Graves and DCI Williams returned to the incident room and sat down again at their respective desks. There was no indication what they had been talking about.

'Are we going to start telephoning the heads of state around the world?' asked Rick Passmore, who was obviously becoming impatient to leave. 'And if not is there any way in which I can still be of help? I'm getting very tired and need a rest.'

'I don't think we are really at the point of telephoning international leaders,' replied Graves. 'At the moment we have not received the go ahead from our own government and we have precious little information. Your help may be needed in a little while so we would be obliged if you can stick around a bit longer, please.'

'OK,' Passmore reluctantly sat down again. 'I really am getting very tired and would appreciate going home soon.'

Kurt looked at his watch. It was already half an hour past midnight. The three hours given by the abductors would be over in fifteen minutes time and the company in the incident room had not succeeded in contacting many heads of state and showed no sign that they would be able to do so in the time remaining. The officials they had spoken to had been particularly obtuse and disbelieving. It was a difficult pitch to sell....who in their right minds would believe that there were shape-changers, worshipped in ancient times as gods of the rivers and seas, who were perpetrating a campaign against the human race? Kurt's nerves were getting ragged due to the waiting but he could see see that there was nothing he could do but try to be patient. Kurt sat far back in the room. He was dog tired and despite his terrible fears regarding his wife and children he was drooping.

It looked to Kurt as if his suggestion that they should call for a ceasefire with no recriminations on either side was the idea they were going to use rather than the surrender that Passmore had suggested. This was more due to the team's failure in contacting the people they wished to reach rather than because they thought that Kurt was necessarily right but if his wife and children disappeared for ever, possibly devoured by one of the monsters, he would not be able to live with himself. He would always think that it was his own fault.

What was stranger, however, was the way that the creatures had changed their modus operandi. They had shown no sign that they wanted to negotiate previously and suddenly they had taken hostages. It was as if something had happened that had made the monsters change the way they behaved.

Kurt looked round the room at the various police personnel sitting at the desks and at the civilian helpers. Hercules, well-connected but an unknown quantity who had lived under assumed names for centuries. Lah Lah, apparently a wood elf or sprite who was sister-in-law to Hercules. Rick Passmore, a scientist whose estranged lover was killed by someone who looked almost exactly like himself, but who had a cast-iron alibi. Peter Mingan, a werewolf who was acting ambassador for the entire Faerie reality. Had any of these people done something that had changed the way the shape-changers behaved?

Then, of course, you had to consider the police: Superintendent Penny Graves, in charge of the unit leading the investigation, the Detective Chief Inspectors, Williams and Rogers, who were jointly second in command, and Sergeant Sid Johnson who had to do the running around. It was odd that they did not have a flurry of constables helping but that was the way it was. Were they doing something that worried the shape-changers?

As Kurt wearily looked round he felt a change occur in the room, Everything had become more weird. It occurred to him that anybody in the room, apart from himself, could be a shape-changer. Even the furniture could be shape-changers if they could successfully imitate an armchair.

No, that's ridiculous, thought Kurt. *An armchair that nobody is looking at is one thing but a desk with a totally flat surface or a chair with spindly legs...they wouldn't be able to copy that. But the personnel....that is a different matter.*

Kurt looked at Rick Passmore. Sure enough his features were changing. He was a monster. Kurt glanced at Dan Williams, the policeman had saved him from the creatures but even he was changing into a tubular structure with long tentacles. The huge hero Hercules was not what he seemed, his body was melting and changing before Kurt's very eyes. Then Penny Graves transformed into the largest monster of the lot, flowed across the room and started to swallow Kurt's feet. Kurt felt no pain then bang! His head hit the desk in front of him and Kurt woke up. Despite all his fears his tiredness had got the better of him and he had fallen to sleep and into a really bad dream.

Waking was not much better: he was back in a nightmare reality. His beautiful wife Sally was missing, along with his fabulous twins and there were moments only left before their time was up. He glanced at his watch. Although his dream had seemed to last for hours only a couple of minutes had passed.

The nightmare had, however, left something in his mind. Maybe one of the leaders of the monsters really was in the room with them? Maybe that was the change in circumstances that had prompted the shape-changers to alter their activity?

Kurt resolved to talk to Penny Graves about this. It was a new way of looking at the situation. Before he could do so two telephones rang simultaneously and both Williams and Rogers clamped receivers to their ears. They both waved their hands in a negative manner and shook their heads indicating that it was not the kidnappers on the line. The conversations were short and Williams reported first.

'Plymouth police chasing the Spots Utility Vehicle have traced it onto the motorway system and to the outskirts of Bristol. They did this with a variety of digital cameras and photographs show two police in the front and an adult woman plus two children in the back .'

'Have they followed them into Bristol? Do they know where they are?' asked Kurt, animated again despite his tiredness.

DCI Williams was still listening to the phone.

'Apparently they have just found the car abandoned, ironically enough, here in Bristol in one of our suburbs called Fishponds. Forensics are looking at the vehicle. No reports of stolen cars from that area,' remarked Williams.

'I've also got some interesting news,' stated Jim Rogers. 'The forensic scientists who have been analysing the pools of water in the Clifton hotel have discovered traces of DNA.'

'What type of DNA have they found?' asked Kurt, the thought of talking to the detective superintendent put on hold for the moment.

'A previously unknown member of the molluscan class Cephalopoda, subclass Coleoidea,' stated Rogers, taking care when pronouncing the words. 'That is the nearest they can get.'

'Well done my lad,' said Hercules, clapping Kurt on the back. 'You were right. They are some kind of octopus or squid. Good guess on your part.'

'They also noted ink-like material in the water,' added Rogers. 'Suggesting that the fluid had been lost because the shape-changer was frightened and had to make an emergency change in shape.'

'So they might change in other circumstances without leaving fluid?' asked Penny Graves.

'Perhaps,' agreed Rogers. 'That is not definitely known.'

'It would have to be a new species to science,' stated Kurt Collins.

'Why is that?' asked Dr. Passmore.

'There are no known freshwater cephalopods,' replied the marine biologist. 'Something that has long been a bit of a mystery.'

'Have there been any explanations given?' asked Rogers.

'It's always been thought that they never developed the means to deal with the osmotic change to freshwater,' answered Kurt.

Most of the team in the incident room looked blank on hearing Kurt's explanation but Hercules, to the surprise of all in the room, was totally au fait with the terminology.

'Clearly these creatures must have a sufficiently developed sodium pump,' he nodded.

'And in addition we know they use charm, a form of magic, and they would need a mechanism for manipulating that,' stated Peter Mingan.

'They did mention that there were some unusually active

magnetite material in the debris,' reported Rogers. 'Could that be part of it?'

'Lord James Scott discovered that magnetic monopoles are integral in the manipulation of magic and that magnets or lodestones could be used to detect it,' answered Peter the werewolf.

'So does that mean yes?' asked Williams, trying to follow all of the jargon.

The werewolf looked as if he was about to howl with laughter then simply nodded his head.

'They've got that information very quickly,' said Rick Passmore. 'What amazes me is that you got the laboratory to do the work at this time of night.'

He very pointedly looked at his watch. Kurt recalled that Rick had already indicated he wanted to leave. It suddenly became imperative to Kurt that he spoke to Penny Graves about his ideas. But once again before he could do so the telephone rang. This time it was the shape-changing abductors.

'You have not responded to our demands and the girl called Milly will die first,' said the spokesman.

'Stop, stop!' cried Rogers. 'We have a suggestion.'

'Go ahead,' replied the shape-changer. 'We will listen.'

'We declare a ceasefire, no recriminations on either side and any prisoners you have taken to be released unharmed. In return, when you have shown good faith, we solemnly pledge that we will call the heads of state and pull all the strings we can to stop pollution of waterways and seas. The only reason we have not got very far as yet is that we have been having trouble getting through to the leaders.'

'That is a weak suggestion but we will give you fifteen minutes to come up with a better suggestion,' replied the shape-changer.

The line went dead.

Kurt ran over to Penny.

'I need to speak to you privately,' he quietly told her.

'Certainly,' she replied. 'You're the second person to want to do that within the hour.'

They walked into the corridor and Penny closed the door so that the others would not hear.

'What do you want to tell me?' asked Penny.

'It has occurred to me that kidnapping my wife and children is not the way that these creatures normally act,' he answered.

'OK,' replied Penny. 'That much is obvious.'

'So something has changed and we must be involved in that something.'

'What do you mean by saying we must be involved?'

'I mean that our team has been instrumental in changing their modus operandi.'

'Sounds plausible but what do you think has made that happen?'

'Two things. Number one is the fact that we have proven their existence. That is something that has never happened before.'

'Right. A very significant point.'

'But I don't think that is all,' surmised Kurt. 'I believe that their leader is near here and may actually be one of the people in the incident room.'

'That's a very interesting conclusion. Why do you think that?'

'Any general worth his salt would want to be near the site of action,' answered Kurt. 'And if the leader were to be one of us, he or she might be passing information back to the kidnappers. Alternatively the kidnappers might believe that our team has captured the leader.'

'Or possibly both,' replied Penny. 'Maybe the leader or someone close to him is able to sneak little bits of information to them and they still believe that he is not free to leave.'

'How could that happen?' asked Kurt.

'If they knew that their leader would never normally bother

to help us they might think that he was with us under duress,' suggested Penny. 'Perhaps the connection is via telepathy, something which is notoriously patchy and unreliable. Do you have any idea which one it might be?'

'I don't,' replied Kurt. 'It could be almost anyone, including yourself.'

'I can tell you now that Dan Williams has confided in me that he is convinced that information is leaking directly from our incident room to the abductors. He cited several occasions where they should not have known things that they did know.'

'As for example when they knew that Hercules had the telephone numbers of world leaders?' suggested Kurt.

'Good example,' agreed Penny Graves.

The door swung open.

'Fifteen minutes is nearly up,' Jim Rogers poked his head round the portal.

'We're just finishing,' replied Graves, then turned back to Kurt when the door closed again. 'OK. If the next few minutes go badly with the shape-changers I will have to take a chance in order to prevent them from killing your family. Are you with me on that? Can you trust me?'

Kurt looked Penny in the eyes. He could not believe that she was an impostor as that way led to madness.

'Yes,' he finally agreed. 'I do trust you and I trust your judgement.'

They re-entered the incident room just as the telephone rang. Jim Rogers took the call and nodded his head as soon as he identified the caller. He then put the phone onto hands-free.

'You have failed so I shall kill the offspring known as Milly,' said the voice on the line. 'I shall swallow her whole.'

Kurt put his head in his hands. It was all going wrong and his children would die.

'If you do that you will be making a grave mistake,' replied

Penny Graves.

'Why?' asked the shape-changer. 'We have given you a chance to change your ways and you have failed. We shall go back to doing things the way we normally do.'

'That would be very foolish,' replied Penny Graves. 'It would be tantamount to declaring war on the human race.'

'We have already declared war on you,' answered the shape-changer.

'In some ways that is true but it was a surreptitious war in which Homo sapiens was not aware of your existence,' countered Penny Graves. 'Now we do know that you exist we shall seek you out and destroy you unless you come to an agreement with us.'

'You are in no position to do that,' replied the shape-changer. 'We shall kill our hostages and then kill you. See how much good your knowledge of our existence does then. Everybody knows that we exist just before they die and it does them no good at all.'

Penny looked round the incident room at the police and the civilians who had been helping her. In particular she caught Kurt's eye and he nodded to her in agreement. She had to play her last card.

'I doubt that you will be so successful without your leader,' she said firmly.

'What do you mean by that?' asked the voice on the line.

'We have your leader in our power. Achelous is the name he calls himself,' bluffed Penny Graves. 'He is the prince of the river gods, father of the sirens and leader of the shape-changers.'

'You do not have him in your power,' contradicted the spokesperson.

'Oh yes we do,' replied Penny Graves. 'And I would like you to reflect on that fact. He is in the room with me right now and we will have to neutralise him if you harm the hostages.'

Penny again looked round the room. Dan Williams looked the least amazed by the announcement but even he looked worried. Jim Rogers and Sid Johnson were aghast, Hercules and Lah Lah were astonished, Rick Passmore looked nonplussed and Kurt looked petrified. Peter Mingan was poised for action, he was stretching his joints in an alarming way as if about to change into a huge wolf. The hairs on his face and on the back of his hands had started to grow and a distinct growl was coming from his throat.

'We shall give you more time,' the shape-changer eventually spoke. 'We do not believe that you have identified or controlled our leader but we need time for confirmation.'

'If you return the hostages I can assure you that we will do all we can to alleviate the problems caused by pollution of rivers and seas,' replied Penny Graves. 'You will not suffer the usual penalties for your past crimes as it is unlikely that the laws we have in place include crimes perpetrated by shape-changers. You are an intelligent species and I really do believe we can work together.'

'Can we expect the same consideration that you have given other intelligent species such as the manatees, the river dolphins or the whales?' asked the shape-changer, clearly speaking sarcastically. 'Or will you start using us for ornaments like you have done the elephants and the lions, eat us as you have done to the chimpanzees and gorillas, or simply outbreed us and destroy us as you did to the Neanderthals and Denisovans?'

The line went dead before Graves could reply.

'That was stupid,' cried Rick Passmore. 'They'll find out that you don't have their leader in captivity then they will kill the hostages.'

He was standing by the small utility sink near where the staff made their tea having earlier opted to washing up the crockery.

'Oh, but we do,' sighed Penny Graves. 'He is standing right in this room with us.'

'Then it must be the sprite,' cried Passmore.

They looked over at the beautiful, young lithe girl with the pointed ears. She smiled back at the company but then morphed into a leech-like shape with a huge mouth which was slobbering fetid saliva.

'Kill her,' cried Passmore. 'She is the leader and she must die.'

Penny Graves stood stock still, hesitating to do anything. She had heard from DCI Williams that Hercules had seen the sprite turn into a monster previously. The sprite had told Hercules that the transformation was an illusion but seeing it in the flesh was quite a different thing and the sprite could have been lying. The creature was huge and it was obvious to anyone that it could swallow a person whole. It was a slightly different colour from the monsters they had seen in the videos but it was obviously of the same species and it certainly did not look illusory...it looked real. Perhaps Penny's idea, as to who the leader of the shape-changers actually was, would prove to be wrong.

Before anybody else could react the werewolf had completed his change from a man into an enormous wolf, bigger than any that Penny or the other members of the team could recall having ever seen. The lycanthrope sprang at the poorly differentiated neck below the huge slobbering maw of the monster that Lah Lah had become but before he could sink his teeth into the creature a strong hand caught him in mid air. The hand was that of the large hero, Hercules.

'Sit down Peter,' ordered Hercules. 'This is not the leader and I will not have her harmed.'

The huge wolf turned back into the naked, hairy man known as Mingan.

'How do you know that, demigod?' growled the werewolf. 'Put me down and tell me.'

'I just do, lad,' answered the huge hero in a powerful voice that broached no argument. 'I'll tell you the reasons later.'

Mingan sat down wearily, watching developments and sniffing the air. Hercules was right. The smell of the river did not come from the area the transformed sprite occupied but from further away in the room.

'Change her back,' ordered Penny Graves. 'We know that she is not the shape-changer.'

She had noticed the same sign that Hercules had...despite the emergency change in shape that Lah Lah had undergone there was no pool of water at her feet.

'Dr. Rick Passmore I would like you to sit down away from the sink,' suggested Penny Graves.

'Why should I do that?' asked Passmore. 'I'm busy clearing up.'

'Very commendable,' nodded Graves. 'But there is more to it than that isn't there?'

'Whatever do you mean?' asked the tall, smooth scientist. 'What are you getting at Superintendent Graves?'

'You gain strength from the water, don't you Achelous?'

'Why are you saying such a thing, Penny, why?'

'You're the prince of the river gods, aren't you Dr. Passmore? We've even got images of you engulfing poor Marianne Foxleigh.'

'We've gone into all that, Penny. You know we have. I was at a dinner in Bristol and everybody saw me there. You even have photographic evidence.'

'A cast-iron alibi if there was just one shape-changer, Dr. Passmore, but meaningless if there are two.'

'Why are you saying my alibi is meaningless?' Passmore was becoming agitated and had not moved away from the sink. In fact the water was running over and wetting the floor of the incident room.

'I repeat...please step away from that sink.'

'No!' replied Passmore flatly refusing to do so.

Hercules lifted his enormous muscular frame from the chair on which he had gently perched his massive bulk. Peter Mingan flexed his muscles ready for another quick change and action. The sprite had reappeared from the illusionary monster that had been inflicted on her and flitted on top of one of the desks to the side of the scientist, watching him most closely.

'Why are you picking on me?' cried the scientist. 'I am here of my own free will helping you!'

'You may well have come in by your own free will but you won't go out that way,' growled DCI Williams, who also looked very menacing when he stood up and flexed his muscles.

Jim Rogers and Sid Johnson took tasers from their desks and pointed them at the scientist.

'I think you can put those away,' grinned Penny Graves, completely calm in the face of imminent battle. 'I doubt if they would work on this creature.'

'You are right,' said Dr. Passmore in a very unctuous tone. 'Thank you Penny. I knew you would see reason. Now all you have to do is open the door and let me out then nobody will get hurt.'

'Your charm will not work on me,' replied Penny. 'Just as it has not been working all evening. I already have earplugs in my ears. Such a simple remedy as suggested by Sergeant Johnson and yet it works.'

'Charm is not my only power,' screamed the scientist, changing shape into a huge tubular structure with massive tentacles. The monster was vastly larger than anyone had expected given the slim form of the scientist.

'You are of course right,' rumbled the voice from the huge maw. 'I am the god of the river. But the knowledge will do you no good. You shall all die and we shall continue our campaign.'

Penny signalled with her hand to Dan Williams and he tried to get round behind the monster to turn off the taps of the overflowing sink. Achelous hit him away from the water and the sink continued to overflow.

'What made you think that I was the god?' asked Achelous.

'Was it my beauty?'

'No,' replied Penny. 'I thought that it ought to be you all along. It was so obvious but your double bluff using another shape-changer as yourself at the Pink Elephant dinner caught me out for a while. But why did you kill Marianne Foxleigh and where is the real Dr. Passmore?'

The monster shook with mirth.

'The real Foxleigh and the real Passmore died five years ago. We took their place.'

'I get it,' cried Kurt Collins. 'Foxleigh was in fact your queen and you killed her because she would not obey you and she was getting too high a profile as a human being. You were jealous.'

'Jealous?' burbled the monster. 'A god is not jealous. She had forgotten who she really was and thus endangered the campaign. So she had to die.'

'But why did you tell us she was missing?' asked Rogers. 'You were the one who reported her disappearance.'

'It's simple,' interjected Penny. 'He knew we were investigating the missing professionals and he wanted to be at the site of the action so that he could misinform us and inform the other shape-changers.'

'Even as you speak they are on their way here,' stated the monster.

'How can you be river gods?' asked Sid Johnson. 'Where have you been all these years?'

'We were very active when Hercules was first abroad,' replied the massive creature, growing in strength and size all the time.

'Maybe but we've not seen hide nor hair of you since then,' muttered Johnson unable to get out of the police habit of pushing for an answer to his questions. 'Surely the marine specialists would have discovered your species years ago if you really existed.'

Penny Graves looked at Johnson as if to warn him from pursuing the questioning. This was a highly intelligent and powerful creature that made a habit of eating human beings. But the monster simply shook with disturbing ripples of jelly-like flesh....it was actually laughing at Johnson!

'You surely not questioning my existence?' the huge maw burbled with evil mirth.

'But where were you for the last two or three thousand years?' asked Johnson, clearly not picking up on his boss's unspoken communication. 'Scientists would surely have discovered your existence and fishermen would have seen you.'

'We are an ancient species,' replied the huge shape-changer. 'We had been around for hundreds of millions of years before the first human beings appeared.'

'How old are you?' asked Dan Williams, having decided that keeping the creature talking may give them the team a chance to counter the monster. Penny Graves tried to dissuade him because she had noticed that every minute the creature was growing larger.

'I am at least three times as old as Hercules,' boasted the monster.

'But you still haven't told me where you were all this time?' asked Johnson. Penny Graves shook her head and gave up on her unequal task of trying to stop her policemen from asking questions.

'I will tell you my story before I kill you,' slobbered the ugly monster. 'Most cephalopods live short lives, perhaps three of four years. Even the North Pacific giant octopus, which can reach thirty feet in length, lives only for five years or so.'

The monster was still apparently enlarging as it spoke.

'This is unfortunate,' continued the massive orifice. 'As they are very intelligent and would otherwise rule the world rather than human beings. We, you can call us Cephalopodia deus if you like, are different.'

'I can tell that,' growled Hercules. 'You can live out of water for a start.'

'More than that,' spat the giant gullet. 'We are virtually immortal knowing no senescence.'

'Senescence?' Johnson queried the term.

'Deterioration with age,' sighed the monster. 'We do not age though we can be killed. We have this form of immortality because we tapped the thaumaturgical force in the rivers and seas. We used river magic to become gods.'

'Is there a god for every river?' asked Dan Williams.

'Only the largest rivers and even some of those have gone,' the creature was definitely sad. 'For millennia the magical power of rivers has been waning. Human beings and their helpers have done this by firstly splitting Faerie from the Earth and then physically damming, barraging and taming all the rivers and streams. This has worsened hugely with pollution and poisoning, dumping of toxic waste, cleaning out of radioactive debris....the list goes on and on. Fishing! You consider that to be a sport but then send out huge ships scraping everything from the bottom of the sea and destroying the very habitat you are relying on to make a living. You are ridiculous.'

The huge monster stopped talking and waved his huge tentacles around, able to reach any part of the room from where it was standing. Then it started its narrative again.

'There is only one river god and one goddess per river. Our offspring are the sirens as you have already concluded but they do not become gods unless the patriarch or matriarch dies. The power of the river then transfers to the next in line.'

'If you were here all the time why didn't our scientists notice you?' Sid Johnson appeared to be obsessed by the question.

'We were here but our powers had decreased due to the effects of human beings,' replied the shape-changer. 'We barely hung in, using our shape-changing abilities and our magical charm to avoid detection, but we just about survived. Gone were the glory days when we could sit out on the rocks luring the sailors to their death. We were the lorelei, the mermaids and the sirens. In Scotland we were the maighdean na tuinne and ceasg and sometimes the monsters in the lochs. In Ireland we were known as the Merrow. What destruction of ships we caused and what fun that was!'

The team in the incident room looked on at the creature, any pity for it having disappeared. This monster was glorying in its memories of drowning sailors!

'But more and more we had to hide ourselves away, looking like fishes or large stones, mimicking the appearance of semi-intelligent species like the dugong. Can you imagine how galling that was? Your fishermen spotted us many times but they were not believed. Your scientists? Pah!'

The giant creature spat a large ball of mucous from its maw, just missing a disgruntled Hercules. Two giant eyeballs on pseudopodia were projecting from the top of the creature and scanning the people in the room with a baleful glare of antagonistic hate.

'Scientists never believe things even when they are right in front of their very eyes,' the monster was speaking again. 'They think they know everything when they only know a small percent of what there is to know. They have only just realised that the Archaea exist and they represent twenty percent of the Earth's biomass! They have just realised, using DNA analysis of sea water, that there are thousands if not millions of species they did not know existed. So the fact that the scientists did not discover our existence should give you no surprise at all.'

The eyes swivelled around looking at each of the occupants of the room in turn then fixed on Penny Graves.

'And now I will start eating you!' exclaimed the huge cephalopod. 'You shall go first as you are the leader.'

'Stop, stop,' cried Penny Graves. 'Tell us first what changed. How did you become more powerful again?'

'How?' cried the monster. 'Isn't that obvious? The two worlds collided at Parsifal X's command and magical forces returned to Earth. Our numbers were much diminished and many of us had become tame or humanised, controlled by Homo sapiens. The giant Colorado river, dammed so it is only a trickle and the god has died. The Nile is weakened. The huge Yangtze, dammed, polluted and poisoned. She is almost dead. But I remain and so do many others and we are helped by our offspring. But now I really must eat. I have grown and I need sustenance.'

A giant tentacle swept across the room towards Penny Graves. Hercules leapt onto the huge appendage and wrestled it away from the female detective. The flexible limb wrapped itself around Hercules and squeezed ever tighter. The demigod fought valiantly back and several more tentacles were recruited to the task of crushing the breath from the hero.

'I've always hated you Hercules,' rumbled the maw. 'The river sprite should have been mine. You cheated when you fought me.'

'Get over it, monster,' cried the hero, twisting one limb away only to have to battle the next which had now got a stranglehold on his neck.

Through the air flew the form of the huge wolf. The magical lycanthrope from Faerie sank its teeth into the tentacle that was throttling the ancient Greek hero only to be tossed to one side by yet another massive coiling limb.

Dan Williams was doing well holding down a rather smaller tentacle and Rogers was assisting both Penny Graves and Sid Johnson as they held down another.

Lah Lah nimbly jumped over the tops of the desks to a frightened Kurt Collins.

'Help me get to the sink,' she demanded. 'Come on. We have to do this to save your family.'

Shaking himself out of his funk Collins distracted the monster by throwing pens, rulers, calculators, anything that came to hand at the huge, baleful eyes of the monster. Finally he threw a bottle of ink that must have lain in a cupboard for years. The cap came off and the ink ran wild spreading over the malformed head of the cephalopod.

The monster turned its enormous mass towards Collins and actually laughed.

'You think that is impressive, puny human?' cried the river god. 'Try this for ink!'

A massive jet of black ink erupted from the creature and spread back towards Collins. In that instant the sprite bounced nimbly over the river god's head and turned off the taps. Almost instantly the creature began to decrease in size. It turned round towards the sink to be confronted by a golden dragon at least as large as itself. The octopoid creature reared back in alarm and tried to run towards the window, moving swiftly on its unencumbered tentacles. Hercules was still hanging on as the two of them burst through the glass and down two stories to the ground below. The creature turned into a massive snake which coiled itself around Hercules' body. The Greek hero grabbed the snake's tail and thrust it deep into its own mouth. The creature coughed, twisted away and reformed as a giant bull that put its head down and charge at the hero. Dancing to one side Hercules grabbed at the bull's head and, as in the legends, took hold of one of the horns. Twisting it with a mighty tug Hercules detached the horn from the head of the river god. The bull turned back into a man-shape and lay panting on the ground.

The rest of the company from the incident room had hurried down the stairs out to the front of the building. The uniformed night sergeant had also appeared and sirens could be heard blaring in the distance. The wounded river god was now in completely human form but was missing a foot and an ear.

'You may have wounded me,' hissed Achelous. 'But you will not defeat the other shape-changers and they will soon be here to assist me.'

'I don't think so,' stated Penny Graves as she linked the god's arms together with iron handcuffs. 'You see I sent uniformed police to surround your house and they have been assisted by the SAS.'

'What can they do against an army of shape-changers?' asked the river god.

'They are armed with the very latest defoliants that are harmful to aquatic life and harmless to human beings,' answered Graves. 'I did that as soon as I heard that the kidnappers were heading towards Bristol.'

The creature was losing fluid and gradually passing out.

'Quickly,' ordered Graves. 'Hercules, put pressure on his wounds to stop the flow of plasma then take him to the iron-clad cell in the basement. Johnson, you go with him. Lock him in then turn the fresh water hose on him. We don't want him to die.'

'Why are you trying to save me?' asked the feeble voice of the river god.

'Because my offer was genuine,' replied Penny Graves. 'I do believe that we need to save the rivers and the seas and I do not want to fight you.'

'You are honourable!' exclaimed Achelous. 'You are not like most human beings.'

'I don't know,' replied the female detective. 'I think that most human beings are basically decent and almost all would like to save the rivers and the seas. We just don't know how to go about doing it.'

'Visit me in the cell,' cried the monster as they took him away. 'I can help advise you. We can do a deal.....and Collins.....your family are safe. The other shape-changers particularly liked the young elvers.'

'I will call off the attack on your house if you agree that the shape-changers surrender,' announced Graves.

'I have, by telepathy, already told them to do so,' cried the river god as it disappeared through the door.

'Now we just have to mop up the damage,' remarked Hercules as he carried away the stricken river god. 'It's going to be more difficult than cleaning out the Augean stables.'

'And I need to get this ink off me,' cried Kurt Collins, whose face was dyed a bluish-black. 'My family won't recognise me.'

'Leave it on,' replied Dan Williams. 'It's an improvement.'

'There's just one thing that is confusing me,' said Penny Graves as she stood looking up at the broken windows of the incident room. 'Where did the dragon come from and where did it go to?'

'The river god is not the only one that can spin an illusion,' stated Lah Lah. 'And I happen to do a good impersonation of a dragon.'

The sprite stood looking up at the window with Penny Graves.

'Mind you,' she added. 'It really is just an illusion, not a shape change so it only has shock value.'

'The monster could easily have turned the running water back on then?' asked Penny.

'Of course,' answered Lah Lah. 'But it's all water under the bridge now.'

Epilogue

'I still don't really get it,' said Jim Rogers. 'It was Rick Passmore who called the police to say that his housemate was missing, he also suggested magic was involved and that the people who were missing were involved in work on rivers and seas. Why would he do that if he was the Achelous, the god of the rivers?'

It was several days later and they were sat round a large kitchen table at Dan Williams expensive flat in Bristol.

'And why did he date his own queen, looking like himself? and then....,' Sid Johnson was interrupted.

'And then kill her?' interjected Penny Graves. 'Yes. It is very strange but he obviously wanted to be at the centre of the investigation so that he could influence it.'

'And he tried to put the blame on the fairies,' added Peter Mingan.

'I think he realised that I was onto something when I called the police,' suggested Hercules. 'And he couldn't be sure how much I knew or how much I would recover from the spells that were binding me.'

'I reckon he dated Marianne Foxleigh and did so looking a lot like himself because he knew that she was in love with him,' proposed Lah Lah. 'He was the one who had fallen out of love with her, not the other way round.'

'In fact the yummy date didn't look exactly like Achelous,' reflected Rogers. 'It was a younger, more handsome version.'

'But he could always make himself look younger and more handsome if he wanted to,' Sid Johnson was still puzzling.

'The looks of the people Achelous became are not really significant except in creating a response from people he interacted with,' Penny Graves pointed out. 'He is really a magical shape-changing octopus-like creature, not a man.'

'But he is a fully sentient creature, easily as intelligent as a human being,' countered Hercules. 'And the human race is going to have to come to terms with the idea of giving human rights to more creatures than just themselves.'

'Hear ye, hear ye!' cried Lah Lah, in hearty agreement.

'We are working on it,' replied Penny Graves. 'I have been very active the last two days. I have had consultations at the very highest level. Changes are to be made in the European Convention and the United Nations Declaration of Human Rights.'

'And the pollution and despoilment of rivers and seas?' queried Hercules. 'What has been done about that. I did give you the numbers of the world leaders.'

'And I used the numbers and quoted your name, Harry Clease, very liberally,' replied Graves.

'Because I believe this is a one-off chance to win the goodwill of the river god shape-changers,' Hercules was speaking very seriously. 'If we don't come up with the goods we may not get a second chance. There are likely to be many more shape-changers out there and they are holding fire, waiting to see what we do. If we get it right we can save the rivers, save the seas and pacify the gods. If we get it wrong we will not win next time.'

'But tell me please,' asked Lah Lah. 'Is Achelous really a god?'

'He has more supernatural powers than I do, that's for sure,' remarked Hercules.

'Yeah, but you're only a demigod,' joked the sprite. 'Immortal, maybe, but only half a deity.'

Hercules laughed.

'You can't upset me,' he chuckled. 'I'm just delighted not to be the semi-paralysed Tim Cranbrook, bless his cotton socks and may he rest in peace.'

'Which reminds me,' said Penny Graves. 'Dan, you were going to give me the latest update on the other shape-changers, the raids on the house in Royal York Crescent and the fate of the Collins family.'

'You mean Whittington and the COE of Bedlam?' asked Williams.

'Indeed.'

'They are one and the same person...just one shape changer,' answered Williams. 'The Collins family were all fine and all of the shape-changers resident at the Royal York Crescent house gave themselves up without a struggle.'

'The house was truly amazing,' said Sid Johnson. 'The swimming pool in the basement...I've never seen anything like it. It beats the Eden project.'

'How many shape-changers were residing at the house?' asked Jim Rogers.

'About twenty, including Peter or Dick Whittington, who came out looking like an old man,' replied Williams. 'He claimed to be Old Father Thames but he spent a considerable amount of time in the shape of a big black cat and only changed into the old man when the police arrived at the property and he received the telepathic message to surrender.'

'Dick Whittington masquerading as Puss in Boots!' exclaimed Lah Lah. 'That's priceless.'

'But what could be more London and the mighty Thames than Whittington and his cat?' mused Penny Graves.

'Do you think any of them were there when I first visited Dr. Passmore?' Jim Rogers posed the question to Dan.

'Most of them, I believe,' replied Williams. 'They became armchairs, sofas, coat stands...even a very large amaryllis. A few of them were probably down under the water when I was shown the pool.'

'That is spooky,' shuddered Jim Rogers. 'I must have walked

right past them.'

'So did I,' nodded Williams. 'I don't think I'll be able to look at another amaryllis without thinking of shape-changers or sit in a big soft armchair without believing it might absorb me.'

'So who was Dame Marianne Foxleigh?' asked Lah Lah. 'I know you have decided that she was Achelous's queen but did she come over from Greece, was she from Egypt, the spirit of the river Nile, or what?'

'One of the shape-changers told me that she had a long list of names but that her original name was Hafren or Habren,' answered Williams.

'Habren?' queried Lah Lah. 'That sounds Celtic.'

'Yes,' agreed Williams. 'The latin version is Sabrina and the river is the Sabren.'

'The Severn!' exclaimed Penny Graves. 'That's rather sad.... Dame Marianne Foxleigh was the spirit of the River Severn!'

'And we put a barrage across it,' commented Kurt. 'And in doing so changed her nature and she forgot who she was.'

*

All of the ad hoc team had departed from Dan's flat except for his boss Penny Graves.

'So what do we think we have learnt from this?' asked Penny, leaning forward over the kitchen table and sipping her cup of lemon and ginger tea.

'I've learnt not to underestimate the power of magic,' replied Dan Williams as he poured himself another glass of Thatcher's Gold cider. 'I have to admit that I thought everything had gone back to normal after the last supernatural scare died down but it hasn't.'

'No, it certainly has not,' Penny was contemplative. 'Nothing ever returns to the way it was before. Time is like a great wheel ever moving onwards but just when you think the cycle has been completed, that the place on the wheel has reached the top again and you believe the cycle of events is going to be repeated you find that the ground you are travelling over has changed. The next cycle may be similar but it is never exactly the same.'

'And every now and again it is completely changed,' added Williams. 'And the wheel rolls down an unknown path which is forking into several branches whilst you are steering it from the rear of the vehicle looking backwards at where you have gone and simply guessing where you are going.'

'You don't ever drive like that, do you?' asked Penny Graves, mock seriously.

'No, boss, I don't,' answered Dan. 'But as you had gone into the realms of wild imagining and analogy I thought I might do the same.'

'Fair point,' nodded Penny. 'On a practical note I firmly believe that we need to keep a police unit ready for the detection of supernatural crimes.'

'Fight fire with fire?' suggested Dan. 'We'll have to recruit wielders of magic and the supernatural if we are going to combat hex-powered criminals.'

'I'd like to start with Hercules. Do you think he would join an undercover unit?'

'Do you know boss, he just might do that. He's had considerable experience with the military and he has megawatts of power.'

'And if we could get Lah Lah and Peter Mingan to help on a semi-permanent basis we would have the makings of a great team.'

'A truly great team,' replied Dan.

'Just one last thing about the case that's been confusing me,' said Penny Graves.

'What's that, boss?' asked Dan.

'Everybody who heard the sirens speak or sing was charmed by them except Kurt Collins,' replied Penny.

'True,' Dan Williams nodded his head.

'The only people who were immune were those who had earplugs in,' mused Penny.

'And the warder at Bedlam,' added Williams. 'She didn't seem to be charmed by anybody but then she was profoundly deaf and had hearing aids in both ears.'

'So what do you think kept Collins safe?' asked Penny. 'Was it just his love for his family?'

'I expect it was partly that,' replied Dan. 'But I reckon that there was more to it than that.'

'What?' queried Penny.

'Have you heard the Collins man sing?' enquired Dan.

'No,' admitted Penny.

'It's diabolical. His singing voice is truly awful.'

'And that saved him from the sirens?' Penny was still perplexed. 'Surely he didn't keep them away by singing to them?'

'He did do that according to his story and I'm sure that affected the sirens badly.'

'But that wouldn't explain his own response to the sirens.'

'His singing is so bad that I have only one explanation and it probably is the reason that he was not charmed by the sirens.'

'I get you....' started Penny.

'That's right,' agreed Dan. 'Kurt Collins is completely tone deaf.'

The End

On a serious note:

The environmental concerns in the book are real and thus the story can be viewed as a parable. Rivers, lakes and seas are constantly being polluted and exploited by human activity, fish and other river and sea creatures are hunted to near extinction. It is not known how long this can continue before the cumulative effect is irreversible. Thus if there were such things as the spirits of the rivers and seas it would not be surprising if they rose up against us......we would deserve it.

Cephalopods really are highly intelligent and really can mimic other creatures. Octopuses have been known to squeeze a huge bulk through a very small crack, climb out of their tanks in aquaria, swing across to other receptacles, eat the contents and return to their own tanks. They are quite amazing!

This book is chronologically placed in the Jimmy Scott (JS) universe between *The Witch, the Dragon and the Angel Trilogy* and the *Witches' Brew Trilogy*. The story occurs after *Tsunami* and is thus the fifth book in the Witch trilogy (it's a magical trilogy so that perhaps explains it!). Relevant stories can also be found in the *Ghost Train anthology of short stories* and *Oberon's Bane*.

About the author:

Paul R Goddard was born in Thornton Heath, Croydon, (now part of Greater London) in 1950. After training in medicine for six years and working in London Teaching Hospitals for three years he moved to Bristol with his lovely wife Lois. His first medical paper was published in 1979 and his first text book in 1986. He has written ten textbooks, fourteen novels, an anthology of poetry and around 500 medical papers.

During his medical career Paul won prizes for his medical publications including the Couch Award and the Twining Medal of the Royal College of Radiologists and the Barclay Prize from the British Institute of Radiology, 2002/2003.

His fiction is intended to be mind expanding and provocative and covers broad subjects of good and evil, philosophy and science as well as fast and exciting action in fantasy and science fiction settings. It is suitable for all ages from 11 onwards.

Paul is a Visiting Professor at the University of the West of England, leader of the band Dr Jazz, and enjoys painting in acrylics. He designs the covers of his own books and recently had three pieces of art on display at an exhibition in New York.

From reviews of some of Paul's previous works of fiction:

The Confessions of Saul
***** **Five Stars**

A cracking novel -I couldn't put it down !
From the first gripping page this novel really is an outstanding and exciting read.
Reviewed by JJ Mann

The Writing on the Wall
***** **Five Stars**

I thoroughly enjoyed reading it and look forward to the sequel.
Reviewed by Liz Varley

Reincarnation
***** **Five Stars**

Moved along so quickly that you occasionally had to take a break to eat....and other things.
Reviewed by Alien

Tsunami
***** **Five Stars**

Brilliant Gothic tale handled by a true story telling master...
Reviewed by J. J. Mann